Contents

DEVOTIONS
FOR
WOMEN
IN THE
WORKPLACE

MIRIAM
NEFF

MOODY PRESS
CHICAGO

To my sisters,
Sally Suofy, Nadine Way,
and Linda Jordan:

Women who help me reach
beyond what I can grasp
and feel beyond the familiar

Preface

Balancing the time crunch with the desire to be a growing Christian is a dilemma. My friend Mary Whelchel recommends reading a chapter in Proverbs every day. I followed her advice and found myself absorbing relevant information as a Christian working woman—advice written centuries ago but relevant to my marketplace and life decisions.

This devotional is the product of my wandering through the wisdom book. It is designed to be read with half a chapter consecutively. The time investment will be brief—often a requirement for devotional time of working women. Hopefully, you will be instructed through Proverbs wisdom and encouraged by one working woman's attempt to hear a higher calling.

And speaking of encouragement, thank you Marilyn Cassells, Winnie Christensen, Brigitte Johnson, and Pat Terrel for reading, critiquing, and mentoring.

MIRIAM NEFF

1
Wisdom

The proverbs of Solomon son of David, king of Is-rael: for attaining wisdom and discipline; for un-derstanding words of insight; for acquiring a disciplined and prudent life. (vv. 1-3a)

My colleague broke open a fortune cookie at a convention dinner and read, "Wisdom is joining your local education association." Ahh. If only wisdom were so simply acquired! I would pay my dues and be the first to join. Many organizations give us information we need. Working women network, share ideas on resolving problems, and review research. We learn from others who have faced similar difficulties. The message placed inside the fortune cookie is crisp and concise. Snap. A tiny piece of paper tells us what to do. But wisdom is seldom so easily acquired.

We work in stores, schools, corporations, homes. We work for pay, we volunteer, we serve. Days of opportunity are days of challenge. Opportunity means choices. Where shall we work? What choices do we make with our paychecks? We seldom work alone; relationships can be sublime, ridiculous, near heaven, near hell. Other people can make our work seem like play or a dark cavernous space in our day that we dread entering.

I want a book of wise answers to my questions as a working woman—answers to the old questions, such as how to get along with people—and answers to new questions, such as the role of ethics in a changing marketplace.

Which of us does not wish for more insight as the issues we face become more complex? Proverbs does not promise fortune cookie answers to these dilemmas. It gives us understanding.

We are becoming more disciplined of necessity. Working women still spend many hours on homework. Women working at home face greater expectations combined with volunteer tasks. They, too, find their homework increased. We must neglect the unnecessary for survival. Thankfully, Proverbs promises to help us become disciplined to make those choices. "In his heart a man plans his course, but the Lord determines his steps" (16:9).

Proverbs also promises to help us become prudent. When I hear the word *prudent* I think of my grandaunt Minnie sitting on her front porch swing, pitting and chopping wormy cherries to preserve the usable pieces. The old-fashioned word sounds irrelevant to the modern era. Not so. My dictionary says that a prudent person is shrewd in the management of practical affairs, and that *is* relevant.

Shrewdness in the management of practical affairs: Proverbs 1:8-9 wisely advises me to listen to the previous generation. Managing practical affairs for Aunt Minnie meant using thoroughly everything available, from wormy cherries to worn-out overalls. Many women from her generation mirrored that good lesson, and I can learn from their example. I can fully utilize my computer. Its capabilities exceed what I presently use. During commuting time I can listen to tapes of praise, spiritual teaching, a foreign language, or recorded books and poetry. Yes, I can learn from Proverbs—and from the New Testament (see Ephesians 5:15)—to make the most of every opportunity.

God is interested in teaching me to be prudent. As I look at my surroundings, the technology may be new and the tools complex, or my resources may seem inadequate. But these elements are only things to be managed by people. I still must choose, like Aunt Minnie, to use my resources fully—to be prudent.

Lord, give me wisdom
to be prudent with my resources in my work today
and to discern what is unnecessary in my life.

2
Priorities

Wisdom calls aloud in the street, she raises her voice in the public squares; at the head of the noisy streets she cries out, in the gateways of the city she makes her speech. . . . But whoever listens to me will live in safety and will be at ease, without fear of harm. (vv. 20-21, 33)

My office is the first on a hallway of other counselors' offices and the coffee pot, sandwiched between the rest room and the front outdoor concourse. "Conveniently located," it's called. A vintage typewriter is clacking outside my door, someone is loudly explaining how to catch the late bus, two students are complaining on their way to the counselor's office next door. I strain to hear a parent, pressing the phone into my ear and earring. Fortunately, I can close my door and reduce the decibel level.

Often we work in the midst of high noise levels: airplanes, cars, cleaning equipment, computer printers, even appliances and electronic equipment in our own homes, contribute to the din. Much of what demands our attention is loud, but not important. Yet it fills our ears as well as our days. For wisdom to get our attention, she must call loudly.

In my work, the student who has run away from home and yet comes to school may wait quietly while others with schedule problems or minor clashes with procedures fill my office and take up my time. The fourteen-year-old single mother may fail classes without confrontation and drop out unnoticed while the aggressive challenger consumes my attention.

Wisdom must make her speech in my ear to redirect my hours and energy. Wisdom tells me to tune out the noise from time to time and ask myself, *What is important in my work? What are the goals of my organization? What are my personal goals within my work setting? What are my family goals?*

Wisdom prioritizes in the noisy street. Should this project consume so much time and so many resources, or has it grown out of proportion? If it is worthwhile, is it worth the price? Wisdom calls at the gateway, "Count the cost!" Most of us have limited financial and emotional resources at our disposal. If we listen to wisdom at the gateway, perhaps she will not have to call so loudly when we are in the busy street.

Successful companies are successful because they have a clear mission. We Christian working women need to visualize our mission. What do we want to accomplish in our work? How shall we balance our work and our personal lives? We bring a new perspective to the marketplace. What will that new perspective be? Do we want a "Good Ol' Girls" network? A corporate track that excludes family life? Short-term profits? Tending the squeaky wheel?

Wisdom does not promise us success in terms of money or prestige. It promises us instead that when we follow her lead, we will be at ease, comfortable with the choices we've made based on convictions as clearly as we can implement them at the moment. And to be at ease is a precious commodity for the working woman. It is the commodity of a wise woman.

Lord, help me to listen as I enter the gate
and while I'm in the noisy streets.

3

Decision-making, Stress

For he guards the course of the just and protects the way of his faithful ones. (v. 8)

Our ten-woman team worked in a small office where we assisted clients who were being transferred from one state to another. Relocating quickly meant uprooting children, changing spouses' employment, and disposing of real estate. On a stress barometer, this registers "overload." Clients' stress became our stress as we became long-distance realtors, moving coordinators, and counselors. Our own deadlines and performance expectations and the heavy volume of work taught us well how each team member responded to pressure-cooker working conditions.

Stress impacted our relationships with our friends, our husbands, our children—and with each other. Some of us coped through solitude, or through diversions such as shopping, exercise, or artistic expression. Others coped by "medicating" the problem, or by using drugs and alcohol. We came to know each other well in that small circle as we overheard personal phone calls and observed "morning afters."

I was sometimes saddened by my friends' choices. What brought them relaxation for an evening meant difficulty concentrating the next day. Companions who provided fun and temporary relief from stress were destructive of self-esteem. A relationship that seemed insignificant at the moment took its toll on parenting. As the only one married to her original husband, the only one parenting four children, and, to my knowledge, one of only two Christians on the team, my perspective was different.

Why did my friends make the choices they did? It became obvious to me that women who do not have God's principles as their guide are adrift on stormy and confusing waters. Without a connection to their Creator through His Son, they had only feelings to guide their decisions. They had no dependable truths, no commands, no wise words to guide them. "I will walk about in freedom, for I have sought out your precepts" (Psalm 119:45). Though my independent spirit sometimes balks at direction and my personality likes quick answers that feeling-based decisions provide, I could see in my co-workers the confusion that comes from living without the knowledge of God. Just as an invisible electronic fence prevents our pets from leaving the safety of home, the Word protects us from behavior beyond the safety of God's guidelines. "If you hold to my teaching, you are really my disciples. Then you will know the truth, and the truth will set you free" (John 8:31-32). We are free—within God's hedges.

Feelings-based decisions result in unstable, turbulent life patterns. They do not accommodate the long-term, consistent, relentless needs of children. God's truths provide a course that He guards and protects. As stress increases in the marketplace or in any other area of our lives, we can choose stress relievers within the boundaries of our knowledge of God. Physical activity, changing our routine, or reading for diversion can help. Whether we are working through the fitness routines of a workout video, are running, or are walking, the exercise will benefit our body and emotions. Diversions such as listening to soothing music or watching a flickering fireplace refresh us. If our job

15

is sedentary, physical work such as shoveling snow, scrubbing the kitchen floor, or tending a garden becomes therapeutic. Friends who know us well may suggest ways we can modify our circumstances to relieve stressful times.

We are not guaranteed a trouble-free heaven-on-earth life. Stress will not disappear. What we *are* guaranteed is the opportunity to make choices based on a wisdom beyond our own.

Lord, thank You for the course You provide.
Help me to share it with my co-workers.

4
Moral Discretion

Discretion will protect you and understanding will guard you. (v. 11)

Proverbs repeatedly encourages moral discretion and gives specific guidelines for sexual involvement. Shrewd working women with no claim to Christian principles have implemented this proverb to their professional benefit. I was intrigued in reading Georgie Anne Geyer's book *Buying the Night Flight* to discover that she does not become romantically involved with work colleagues as a personal principle. An international correspondent, reporter, columnist, and author not claiming to live under God's authority had chosen to live by a biblical truth based on its practicality.

Paul tells us in 1 Corinthians 6:18-20 that no other sin affects us like sexual sin. Our society is beginning to reap the consequences of casual sex, of not following God's direction. AIDS has magnetized national attention. Unwanted pregnancies are terminated in abortion, and the presence of unwanted children polarizes political bodies struggling to make policies. We may avoid admitting the cause, but we are being forced to grapple with the results.

Working women who form sexual liaisons in the marketplace reap additional negative results. These include (1) a reputation based on behavior rather than professional competence, (2) a distracting emotional agenda, and (3) the necessity of resolving or dissolving the relationship.

Working women face great temptations and opportunities, but we can count on God's protection when we discreetly and firmly live by His guidelines. We want others to see us as good stewards of our God-given strengths and abilities. We want the emotional freedom to serve ethically in whatever position we fill. We want to make decisions based on responsible thinking, not liaisons. We want relationships that God can bless.

When temptation comes, remember that a positive sense about ourselves comes from using God-given gifts to the greatest extent possible rather than relying on flattery or titillating encounters. Our worth comes from being unique creations loved by the Creator. We do not need to prove ourselves lovable; He loves us unconditionally.

Even with the self-confidence that is really God-confidence, we need to establish safe hedges for our own protection. We need to avoid opportunities for relationships to develop apart from a professional or neutral friendship. We need to ask a close friend to help us be accountable. Revealing a tempting situation to a trusted friend and asking her to hold us accountable, to pray for and with us, and to give us godly encouragement will give us strength greater than our own.

If women who do not live under God's authority profit from moral discretion, how much more should we! Additionally we will have His blessing for obedience.

Lord, thank You for giving me guidelines
that protect and guard me.
Give me discretion to live within them.

5
Discipline

My son, do not despise the Lord's discipline and do not resent his rebuke, because the Lord disciplines those he loves, as a father the son he delights in. (vv. 11-12)

Have you ever been stuck in the wrong job? Have you ever applied for a job that you *knew* would be right—and someone else got it? Sometimes we find ourselves mismatched in our work. Maybe we accepted a job and then discovered it wasn't all it was presented to be. Perhaps we hastily signed on because we needed a paycheck. Maybe we stumbled into the wrong job because we were changing careers or reentering a profession and hadn't yet got our bearings in the new environment.

These mismatches are often God's opportunity to smooth our rough edges, teach us humility, bring new people into our lives, and bring us a host of other wonderful, valuable experiences—although we don't always see it that way at the time.

Proverbs 3:5-6 is a much quoted passage: "Trust in the Lord with all your heart and lean not on your own understanding; in all your ways acknowledge him, and he will make your paths straight." Our human nature usually does not trust another source of guidance until it is absolutely necessary. As long as our idea is working, why trust God's? Often times of frustration are perfect opportunities to trust God in a new way, to learn leaning.

Looking back on my career mismatches, I can see that those times were high frustration but higher learning. The word *discipline* in Scripture means "teaching." God teaches us through our circumstances as well as His Word. Discipline in an unsatisfying job may mean doing the job well though it is monotonous, uninteresting, and our last preference. Scripture tells us if we're faithful with little, God will give us more.

Discipline may mean working in a system or company that isn't our type. Maybe the company is a sleeping giant, and we are an ant in high gear. Maybe the company is intense and highly driven, and we are laid back, low-keyed types who can't work well with "Rocky" music blaring in our ears. Maybe we aren't at all well matched with the other people at our workplace. What can God teach us through such an experience?

During one two-year period, I blundered through four positions in four different places. Looking back, I realize that I learned more during that period of my life than perhaps any other adult season. I learned the discipline of accepting the disappointment of not getting a job for which I was qualified—and the discipline of accepting graciously the person who did! I learned the discipline of working diligently in a poorly organized and occasionally corrupt place. I learned the discipline of recognizing that a workplace can be no better than its people.

Perhaps the greatest lesson we can learn during a mismatch working period is that the God who created us and gave us the gifts, abilities, and strength to work is primarily interested in our growth as Christlike representatives wherever we are. Secondarily He is also vitally interested in utilizing what He has given us. Unused strengths, gifts, and abilities don't glorify

Him, but this is secondary. Sometimes when I feel mismatched in my work, I list my frustrations in a column. In a second column I write what God might teach me from that frustration. Then I write in bold letters across both columns, "The Lord teaches those He loves as a mother a daughter she delights in."

Lord, thank You for Your love
and for counting me teachable.
Thank You for caring enough about my weakness
to give me the opportunity to change.

6
Relationships

Do not withhold good from those who deserve it,
when it is in your power to act. (v. 27)

Imagine a school where students received green checks for every right answer instead of glaring red X's for errors. Imagine a home where children caught doing something right are complimented. Imagine your workplace if people were complimented for good effort and ideas as well as confronted with mistakes. Maybe those statements describe your workplace, home, and school. If so, be thankful; you have a rare environment.

Usually we grease the squeaky wheel, the acting-out child gets the attention, the error gets the mark. Christian working women can change that. We often have power to act that we have not discovered. Power to act does not belong solely to presidents and supervisors. We can do good even if we have no authority over raises and perks.

An accurate, appropriate compliment can change the working atmosphere, as well as a person's attitude. We all have the power to compliment others. We can tell our supervisor what we like about how she worked through a particular problem. Usually people are encouraged when we notice their strengths and tell them what we've observed. Is there a good listener in your workplace? Tell her how that helps you. As an impulsive person, I sometimes seek advice from my co-worker Mary, who is consistent and always seems to observe details I've missed. My compliment lets her know she is appreciated.

I find it especially difficult to compliment someone whose values, personality, or work style differs from mine, but that may be just the compliment that improves the relationship or work atmosphere. I need to remind myself that God created that individual to be different for His glory, not my comfort.

Some women exercise power over paychecks, perks, and benefits. If you have responsibility as well as the power, be fair. To withhold something rightly belonging to another, even though it may seem minor to you, violates this proverb. Delaying the payment of a benefit or reclassifying overtime hours may make your balance sheet look better to your superiors, but not to God.

If our nation's businesses followed this proverb, we would be less litigious. Our policy manuals would be smaller. Ethics would not be the topic of concern and crisis in the business sections of our newspapers. To do good to those who deserve it is one pillar of an ethical marketplace, a preventative pill for lawsuits. The non-Christian may do good because it works as a preventative pill, but we have a higher motive: pleasing God.

Consider what power you have in your workplace to do good. Positive reinforcement strengthens. God promises prosperity to those who keep His commands. Does this mean financial prosperity? Not necessarily. Ethical accountability may be beneficial, but following His commands may also cost you competitive pricing in a corrupt system. The prosperity I am talking about is the prosperity of being spiritually healthy, of pleasing God.

Lord, give me new eyes
to see how I can do good in my workplace.

7
Valuable Possessions

Hold on to instruction, do not let it go; guard it
well, for it is your life. (v. 13)

What we guard shows what we value. We hold tightly to what is important. In the marketplace, that is obvious. We keep what is valuable in fire-proof vaults, under lock and key, and heavily insured. We insure valuable personal possessions such as cars, antiques, and homes. Our living space usually indicates what is important to us. Our wardrobes may include just the right clothing for our jobs at the same time our pantries contain only generic soup. Speaking for myself, my bookcase is overflowing and my car a poor excuse for a vehicle.

Advertisements tell us our success depends on things. Commercials imply that our social success depends on the car we drive, what we drink, and what brands we wear. What if all these things were taken away? Would we be failures? What is really valuable?

Recently an art gallery was destroyed in a Chicago fire. Millions of dollars worth of prints and oils, as well as sculptures and three-dimensional collages blended together in the rubble. Valuable sculpture and the old building's plumbing were indistinguishable from one another after both were subjected to the heat. A fireman sorting through the rubble was overheard to say, "It's hard to tell what was art here."

What if our workplace lost everything in the vault? Our possessions would then be what we had in our minds and hearts, what we knew and were able to do. Our company would be stripped down to the true source of its value as a business: it would succeed on what it could produce or what its people knew.

Proverbs tells us to hold on to instruction because it is our life. Though it sounds drastic, this is practical advice for today's working women. Companies grow and shrink, eliminating positions. Services become unnecessary or transform to fill new markets. People change careers approximately four times during their work years. I suspect the average is higher for women since we tend to invest fewer years in training and are more directly impacted by family stages. What we know becomes worth guarding. Instruction becomes a valuable commodity. To learn becomes an important goal.

What we have in our minds is one of the few possessions that cannot be taken from us. We can lose a contract, but we cannot lose what we know. Our position may become obsolete, but our brain need not.

This proverb tells us that learning includes judgment and common sense. Those are abilities to evaluate what we see and hear before we act. We may not be Einsteins, but we *can* exercise common sense. Judgment is usually impacted by the information available. We can often increase the quality of judgment by getting information, waiting on an important decision until we have the relevant facts.

Just as we can invest time in learning to grow spiritually, so we can invest time in learning about our work. The instruction we pursue may protect us from unemployment. Classes, books, tapes, resource people, and just looking around with open ears can instruct us. This foundation of learning is often what

God uses as a basis to help us acquire wisdom. Then we possess that which cannot be taken away from us, what Proverbs calls "life."

Lord, help me sift through
the things and rubble in my life
and discover what You value.
Help me to be an eager learner.

8

Impulse

Above all else, guard your heart, for it is the well-spring of life. (v. 23)

Impulse. Why did I do that? I said what? Where did that come from? Me? Really! Sometimes we act, react, and make decisions without knowing why. Scripture refers to our heart as an important control center. The Hebrew word, *lebab,* means the totality of our inner nature: emotion, thought, and will. "My heart grew hot within me, and as I meditated, the fire burned; then I spoke with my tongue" (Psalm 39:3). "Out of the overflow of [the] heart [the] mouth speaks" (Luke 6:45). "As a woman thinketh in her heart, so is she" (Proverbs 23:7, my paraphrase). "My heart is set on keeping your decrees to the very end" (Psalm 119:112). We feel, we think, we speak, we become—from the heart.

I wonder how many decisions working women make daily. Yesterday I interacted with fifteen students in my office, made or received twenty-one phone calls involving faculty, parents, students, and other support personnel, participated in one staffing and one meeting. Though I was involved in many interactions, I did not make outcome-producing decisions; in most encounters my input involved a decision as to what role to play, what perspective to take, or what counsel to give. I felt, I thought, I spoke. No wonder Proverbs tells us to guard our heart.

My children have face guards on their watches. These protectors prevent the watches from scratches, smashes, and other damage. God has given working women a heart-guard—His Word, the Bible. Though our reading moments may be few, every verse we read is a heart-guard. When our hearts are cold, they are warmed by His love. When our hearts are proud, they are humbled by knowing we are only what He made us. When our hearts are deceitful, they are confronted by His honesty. When our hearts are fearful, they are reassured by His consistency. When our hearts are burned out, they are renewed by the knowledge that He is the final judge and that a day will come for fairness, reckoning, and rewards.

Though we need heart-guards for all of these conditions, the greatest heart problem would be not to feel at all. There are examples in Scripture of people whose hearts were hardened; their capacity to make wise decisions was removed. Pharaoh challenged God until he became a robot with a heart of stone, an instrument of death. Though our sphere of influence may be much smaller than Pharaoh's and less earthshaking, we vitally need to maintain our healthy decision-making capacity. At work, in our relationships, and when we try to balance our personal budget, we need a thinking, feeling heart. We won't get such a heart by watching the news, studying the stock market, or reading a job evaluation. The Bible is our best source—at times even our only source.

Proverbs says that the heart is the wellspring of life. The water in a spring-fed lake is only as good as its source. Similarly, if we guard our hearts with His Word, we will be self-assured as God's created women. We will value others as people created and loved by God. This God-given capacity for self-assurance will make a difference when the phone rings, the staffing begins, the meetings heat up. Our heart-guard will assure that we will not lose our decision-making capacities.

Impulse. Yes, I did that. Ownership. Yes, that is in me. Now I know that before I spoke and reacted, I felt or thought. I need to guard my control center, protect my well-spring.

Lord, keep my heart tender
through whatever experiences I encounter.
I pledge to wear my heart-guard.

9
Temptation

My son [daughter], pay attention to my wisdom, listen well to my words of insight, that you may maintain discretion and your lips may preserve knowledge. (vv. 1-2)

"I need." "I want." "I owe it to myself." "No one will know." "But in my circumstances, it's justifiable." We feel the same pull to sin today that young men felt toward prostitutes in Solomon's day. Whether our temptation is to sexual sin or to some other indulgence outside God's hedge of safety and instruction, the basic principle is the same.

Many different sins originate from the same inner impulse: "I need." "It makes me feel good." "What he doesn't know won't hurt him."

Temptation sounds sweet and smooth or it wouldn't be tempting. But giving in to temptation is *always* eventually sour and ragged. Sometimes we say to ourselves, *Not so. Not where I work. It pays to use a weighted scale; it pays to give a dishonest report; it pays to court people for personal gain. Sue Doe is having an affair, and she looks happy. I see people doing those things around me, and they're getting ahead.*

David saw the rewards of dishonesty around him, and it angered him just as it angers and frustrates us.

"But as for me, my feet had almost slipped; I had nearly lost my foothold. For I envied the arrogant when I saw the prosperity of the wicked. . . . Surely in vain have I kept my heart pure; in vain have I washed my hands in innocence" (Psalm 73:2-3, 13). Anger gives way to jealousy.

But God allowed David a heart-cleansing glimpse. He saw sin through God's eyes. "When I tried to understand all this, it was oppressive to me till I entered the sanctuary of God; then I understood their final destiny" (vv. 73:16-17). He saw the final judgment, the last opportunity to report, the last weigh-in. Then David was content; he could rest on God's wisdom.

In the sanctuary of God each stands alone. Only our relationship with Him matters. I can't take anything with me to impress Him. An exquisite home at a prestigious address, the right wardrobe, antiques, and material goods must be left outside. Emotional attachments are inconsequential unless they glorify Him. The final consequence of sin is being separated from the only One who knows you, the only One who loves you. Sin equals loneliness and the turbulence of living a mismatch of all you were meant to be.

If only we could see the long-term view of temptation and the results of giving in. Men in Solomon's day wasted their time and their strength and destroyed their family life with prostitutes. Women can do the same today. The positive aspect of meeting people in the workplace can increase temptation. The independence of a paycheck can lead to an attitude of independence from our covenant of marriage.

Sin's penalty does not always come in this life. Let's assume that you are tempted to do something wrong that seemingly carries no immediate negative consequences. Now imagine being in the sanctuary of your sovereign Lord, talking over that action with God, face-to-face, in a conversational manner. Does the action you are tempted to take still seem so harmless? No, obedience is clearly far sweeter than anything temptation can offer.

"Pay attention. Listen," Solomon says. "You don't have to learn the hard way!" Submitting to discipline means learning from someone else's teaching. But we insist on learning from our own painful experience. We hear the instruction but do not obey.

When you are faced with temptation remember that God will supply all of your needs according to His riches (see Philippians 4:19). He knows your needs better than you do. After all, He created you and placed in you those biological, emotional, social, and spiritual needs you experience. You can imagine being in the sanctuary of God and saying with David, "Whom have I in heaven but Thee? And besides Thee, I desire nothing on earth" (Psalm 73:25).

Lord, may my desire to obey You
be the strongest need in my life.

10
No Surprises

*For a man's ways are in full view of the Lord,
and he examines all his paths. (v. 21)*

"I'm tired of my old wardrobe."
"I'd sure feel better driving to work in a new car."
"This room is boring; we need new furniture."
Our culture doesn't appreciate the qualities of age
—in furniture, homes, relationships, or people. We
want youth. I felt this "youth" emphasis one Friday
night in the grocery store as my son and I shopped for
weekly supplies for our family of six. Tired after a week
of work and mentally listing all that needed to happen
on Saturday, I looked and acted the grouch. John tried
to encourage me. "Mom, why don't we buy some hair
color and fix you up like a young person?" Oh, for the
blessings of youth!

We want quarterly profits at the expense of long-
term growth. We want the stimulation of new surroundings for stimulation's sake. We place high value
on how we feel at the moment. And "new" usually
means "better." This philosophy has spilled over into
our relationships, especially romance, love, and marriage. Supposedly the best part is getting acquainted,
the excitement of the honeymoon, the surprises.

Proverbs tells us to value long-term relationships,
to rejoice in our mate for a lifetime. When there are few

surprises left, we are to value the commitment. "Drink from your own cistern, running water from your own well." Water was precious in that culture. Stealing water was a serious crime, like stealing a man's horse in the days of the old West, and the penalty was high. Solomon was illustrating the value of a long-term relationship. To seek comfort or excitement from another's mate is a high crime.

In our society, sin is seen as being less sinful if nobody else knows. The same must have been true in Solomon's day. Proverbs reminds us even when no one else knows, God is present. Though we may succeed in convincing ourselves that sin can be "less sinful," God sees sin as sin. To Him there is no escape; consenting adults both wanted it; neither spouse knew.

Long-term relationships teach us tolerance, forgiveness, commitment, flexibility, and adaptability. The comfort and support of those relationships give us strength to accept new challenges. A comfortable pair of walking shoes makes a new trail appear welcoming. That same comfort soothes us through crisis: no arms comfort like arms that have been there a long time.

God examines all our paths. We frequently see just the step ahead, focusing our attention on acquiring material goods rather than on preserving a relationship, the wealth that money can't buy.

The book of Romans tells us not to be "conformed to this world, but [to be] transformed by the renewing of [our] minds" (12:2; King James Version). To have a renewed mind is to look farther down the path to the benefits of a long-term relationship, to see the value of loving through hard times, of adapting mutually to the surprises life brings, of accepting differences that require patience. Whether this attitude describes a relative, a friend, a co-worker, or your marriage partner, as you mold one another, grow, and adapt, you can take comfort in knowing that all is in full view of the Lord.

34

He sees not only your slips in the path but also your sacrifices, the times when you give up your rights to preserve a relationship.

Lord, help me to see beyond my immediate wants,
to trust You for what the path holds beyond what I can see.

11

Success

Go to the ant, you sluggard; consider its ways and be wise! It has no commander, no overseer or ruler, yet it stores its provisions in summer and gathers its food at harvest. (vv. 6-8)

My encyclopedia tells me that all ants are social insects and that there is great diversity within and between colonies of ants. Some ant colonies are small, numbering as few as 12 members, whereas other colonies have 500,000. There may be as many as twenty-nine types of "individuals" in a colony or as few as three. Ant colonies may be in trees or in the earth, at the timberline or by the seashore, in cities, posh suburbs, run-down districts, or farms.

What a picture of diversity. Though ant "jobs" are diverse, the common denominator of all ant societies is the acquiring of food for all and the continuation of the colony. What can we learn from ants? They have learned to live together. Whether there are three or twenty-nine different functions, ants perform tasks for the benefit of the colony. Visualize two slugs balancing a tasty morsel as they slither to their home site—it's a ridiculous picture. However, it is easy to remember seeing two tiny ants carrying food five times their size, turning, walking backward, and climbing obstacles to reach their destination. Ants accommodate differences because it benefits the colony.

I think God would be glorified if women who work outside the home and women who've chosen to work in and/or from their homes cooperated like ants. Yet because of our insecurities, we sometimes spend too much time justifying and defending what we're doing —why we have chosen to work outside our homes, or why we have chosen to work in our homes. Why can't we accept our diversity and work toward the common goal of multiplying and subduing the earth, the charge God gave to Adam and Eve? We need the energy we're wasting on self-defense to carry out our diversified tasks.

Ants are future-oriented. They work now for the future. They store food, working industriously while it's available. Sometimes I wish God would give me that purposefulness. I prefer to procrastinate about crucial but difficult tasks, wasting my time on chores that are immediately available to do but are of less importance. That's why God tells me to consider the ant. He gave me the brain to follow the ant's example, even though it's not my nature.

Ants tolerate and accept parasites that do not harm them, but they protect themselves from parasites that would drag them down. We working women might consider this lesson: there is a time to carry others and a time to insist that they function on their own.

Ants have no rulers. Even their queens do not rule. Why? It is because ants naturally work independently toward a common goal. Rulers are unnecessary in their communities. We do need rulers, however, for the members of our community compete with one another. Our competitive human nature can learn from the ant.

The ant has another exemplary characteristic. She is a self-starter. Proverbs tells us that the sluggard wants a little more sleep, a little more hand-folding time (see Proverbs 6:1-11). You and I, like the ant, don't have that luxury. We need to keep working. Our motivation need not be the same as the ant's, however. The ant is motivated by the need for food, but we can be motivated by the desire to glorify God. When immediate rewards seem insignificant, we can refresh ourselves in the knowledge that God will examine the harvest.

Lord help me to be a self-starter,
to accept others' differences,
and to work toward Your goals.

12
Ethics

*There are six things the Lord hates, seven that
are detestable to him: Haughty eyes, a lying
tongue, hands that shed innocent blood, a heart
that devises wicked schemes, feet that are quick
to rush into evil, a false witness who pours out
lies and a man who stirs up dissension among
brothers. (vv. 16-19)*

We recently drove by the Watergate complex in
Washington, D.C. Though a number of years have
passed since the scandal took place that imprisoned
government officials, ruined careers, and removed a
president from office, the site is still famous. Paper fall-
out of the depositions related to that scandal could fill
rooms, the court proceedings filled months, and the
repercussions, especially for those found guilty, last a
lifetime.

Watergate was caused by the desire for power. As
we look at God's hate list, it seems to me that the desire for power puts each into motion.

Haughty eyes. "I'm better than you. I'll look down
on you. I'll use you."

A lying tongue. "The truth doesn't make me look
as good as this modification will."

Hands that shed innocent blood. "This person—
her time, her future, perhaps even her life—is not as
valuable as mine."

A heart that devises wicked schemes. "The unfolding of events would be more advantageous to me if they were manipulated a bit—to serve the cause, of course!"

Feet that are quick to rush into evil. "I'll get what I want—faster. Why wait when I can push the events?"

A false witness who pours out lies. "Lying for myself is not enough. I'll profit by lying for another. Thwarting justice? What's that?"

A woman who stirs up dissension among sisters. "I see friction, a sparking rub that I can fan into a profitable flame."

God does not object to humans' exercising power. He gave us dominion over His whole creation. But power is ultimately His; it is ours only on loan, blessed if used fairly for His purposes. To desire power for our own purposes is to reject that our future, our success, is at His disposal. "Commit to the Lord whatever you do, and your plans will succeed" (16:3). "In everything you do, put God first, and he will direct you and crown your efforts with success" (3:6). What a contrast to using God's hate list to manipulate events so that we might acquire personal power.

The Watergate complex will eventually crumble as will all the buildings, monuments, and memorials in our capital. Depositions and court records will eventually be shredded or burned, or turn yellow with age. Though the events of the Watergate scandal shook lives, governments, and nations, they will be insignificant in eternity. Though the powermongers of Washington shuddered at the prospect of information leaks and scrambled for legal protection, a bigger, far more significant revelation is coming.

If we are tempted in our workplace to use a hate list, we should remember that power so gained is pointless. God cannot **bless** such efforts, whether in attitude, speech, or action, even though we may feel that the goal for which they were employed is noble. In our daily lives, as we are open, fair, honest, patient, and peacemakers, God will clear a path and will exercise His power. We need none of our own.

Though some Watergate information was leaked and more was subpoenaed, we may still not know all the facts concerning the incident. In eternity the whole of each life will be made public. I suspect that some of the world's powerful people will shrink and some of the "nobodies" stand tall.

Lord, guide me to appropriate Your power on earth without siphoning any for my purposes.

13
Obedience

My son, keep my words and store up my commands within you. Keep my commands and you will live; guard my teachings as the apple of your eye. (vv. 1-2)

The Hebrew word for "command" refers to the terms of a contract in a deed of purchase for a plot of land. The word is also used by the wisdom school for the instruction of a teacher to his pupil. Commands are the particular conditions of covenant. The same word is used for the Ten Commandments (cf. Exodus 24:12).

I don't like the word. *Commands.* I see a finger pointing at me, a source of authority of which I am skeptical. But I sense something different in God's commands. His contract with me includes investment on His part and investment on my part—mutuality. He and I have a covenant. He has promised me an eternity in a wonderful, comfortable, beautiful, and safe place with my most favorite Person. At present He gives me a sense of positiveness, self-esteem (or more accurately, God-esteem) because He created me like Himself. That is His part.

My part seems quite meager in comparison. My covenant is just to be. That's all. This is a hard concept to grasp in our doing, earning society. But that is all that is required of me in the covenant. Just to *be*, just to be *His*. The commands are guidelines for my benefit in the covenant. They are proverbs; they are promises. To the extent that I learn them and live by them, I will receive benefits proportionately.

Are they black and white, always guaranteed? No. We live in a flawed world. We are humans, and we live with other humans. Our own sins trip us up, and others' sins trip us, too. God's commands are general. The more closely we follow them as individuals and as nations, the more fully He is able to bless us. But in this life, in our nation, in our workplaces, the covenant will never be complete, the commands will never be fully followed. Sin has existed in our world for too long.

Meanwhile, through His commands, I see God lovingly instructing me on the dilemmas of life, giving guidelines to follow in making decisions. Studying these commands, I see the following:

1. They are clearly revealed. We do not need to guess what they are; God speaks directly in them.

2. God reaches toward us. I am continually amazed that God takes the initiative toward me for my good. No other authority has so positively, aggressively, pro-actively worked to bring out the best in me.

3. His commands are true. Obeying His commands removes ethical inconsistencies.

4. His commands are reliable. They are not memos to be rescinded tomorrow by a new command. There is no "this directive supersedes other directives" quality to them. Thankfully, God is reliable.

5. They are righteous. To be without partiality is a rare quality for humans in authority.

6. They give insight into meaning of life so that we can live our lives to the fullest. His commands expand our world rather than constrict it.

No finger points at me. Strong arms reach out to support me. The commands are precious to me. I *want* to follow them. I *want* to guard them. "Say to wisdom,

'You are my sister'" (v. 4). My three sisters are supportive, caring, nonthreatening, the three women who know my weaknesses, my greatest sins, my moments of humiliation. I can embrace God's commands the way I hug Sally, Nadine, and Linda. Our embrace is not one of naïveté or superficial tolerance but a bear hug of body, soul, and mind. "Now all has been heard; here is the conclusion of the matter: Fear God, and keep his commandments; for this is the whole duty of man" (Ecclesiastes 12:13).

Lord, when I see Your investment in our mutual covenant, I want to hug Your commands like sisters.

14
Wanting Wisdom

I, wisdom, dwell together with prudence; I possess knowledge and discretion. . . . I love those who love me, and those who seek me find me. . . . My fruit is better than fine gold; what I yield surpasses choice silver. (vv. 12, 17, 19)

Once intruders looking only for choice silver robbed our home. They left a silver-plated tea set strewn across the floor, but took sterling flatware. They ripped tiny sterling commemorative spoons from their wall rack, but left cameras and radios behind. They were discerning. They knew what they wanted.

Proverbs tells us that instruction is better than silver, knowledge better than gold. Wisdom is more precious than rubies. We cannot exchange wisdom as a gift or steal it. We must desire wisdom and seek it out.

What effort am I willing to exert in order to get what I want? Effort directed toward gaining wisdom never goes unrewarded. Burglars may enter a house in which there is no silver, but Proverbs tells us that those who seek wisdom will find her, a discovery better than choice silver or fine gold.

Wisdom dwells with prudence. There's that old-fashioned word again, still brimming with relevance. Looking at this word throughout Proverbs, we learn that the prudent woman does not flaunt her knowledge (12:23). The co-worker who acts as though she knows it all is usually not admired. The prudent woman simply acts with knowledge (14:8). She values being informed, and her decisions show it. Ignorance in the marketplace is disaster, not bliss. Moreover, the prudent woman ignores an insult (12:16). She weighs it in her mind to profit if the insult is valid or a necessary rebuke, but she does not react defensively. If the insult is undeserved, she may be equally quiet because she needs no defense.

The prudent woman looks where she is going (14:15). She does not suffer from the ostrich complex. She foresees danger and acts appropriately (23:3; 27:12). We cannot take steps to avoid danger if we do not see what is ahead. The Scarlet O'Hara approach, "I'll worry about that tomorrow," works only if someone is available to rescue you. Most working women do not have such a luxury; in fact they would prefer not to be helpless and in need of a rescuer. In our work we know that ignoring a potential problem today may result in a crisis tomorrow. To avoid those situations, we need real glasses, not rose-colored ones. The prudent woman is crowned with knowledge (14:18). No wonder she is seen as a shrewd lady expertly managing her daily affairs.

I sometimes wish that acquiring God's wisdom guaranteed gold and silver in my possession. But wisdom does not guarantee riches. Few of us will have wealth. Even if we did, I can testify that it is easily lost. We may desire to have the genius and leadership to work miracles in our workplace, but the results would likely be short-lived. Better to be wise women possessing prudence, working consistently a day, a month, a year at a time.

Proverbs tells us that the fruit of wisdom is better than riches that can be stolen. I do not know what reward God will bring as the fruit of wisdom. After the robbery we ate our Thanksgiving feast with plastic forks and knives. We enjoyed the fruit of thankfulness for each other, for health, and for the ability to enjoy a delicious meal. That was more precious than fine silver.

Lord, help me find wisdom.

15
The Craftsman

Then I [wisdom] was the craftsman at his side. I was filled with delight day after day, rejoicing always in his presence, rejoicing in his whole world and delighting in mankind. (vv. 30-31)

Sometimes I'm skeptical of depending on God's wisdom. If you are a naturally trusting woman, you will not understand this. But some of us are always looking for a better idea, for our own formula. Like an unfettered racehorse or a hunting dog picking up a new scent, we're off. We trust our instincts and impulses readily and view the rest of the world with a question mark soaked in skepticism. *How could God know better? How could wisdom reveal a better way?* we ask ourselves. When I sense my skepticism of godly wisdom, I reread this portion of Proverbs. Wisdom was at God's side during creation; he served as God's craftsman, the engraver. God created; wisdom carved. God called matter into existence; wisdom molded.

Wisdom enabled. Water doesn't fall off the underside of the world, a phenomenon that baffles my simple mind. Wisdom secured the fountains of the deep. Have you ever seen the power of water in a hurricane? the momentum of floodwaters? felt the undertow of a tide? God's power can control water; He gave the sea boundaries so that it could not overstep His command. His power can settle mountains. Whether in a speeding landslide, torrential volcano, or the slow but unstoppable moving glacier, mountain-moving is not the stuff of the ignorant or weak. A source of power this great sounds reliable even to skeptics like me.

I have a bowl-shaped rock that is among my favorite treasures from childhood. I discovered it when I was wading upstream on our southern Indiana farm forty years ago. It may be a fossilized knot from a tree; I don't know the powers or years that shaped it so uniquely. My rock bowl has held wild roses, Christmas candy, baby cotton swabs, writing utensils, and paper clips. It reminds me that I can trust God's wisdom to make something usable of the unlikely—a rock bowl.

Usually when a person is ready to learn, a teacher appears. Wisdom reaches toward me in my little world, offering me more than I could ever hope to create on my own. God offers me His craftsman, Wisdom, to engrave my world, to shape the forces in my life, my work, and my relationships.

Recently I was frustrated because a student who desperately needed one of our resources could not receive assistance because of a technicality. How often does Jesus look at me in similar frustration. He has a way, but my stubborn mind-set closes the alternative. I miss the opportunity, waste the resource.

Yet God's craftsman, Wisdom, looks at me with delight. Wisdom rejoiced to be at God's side and delighted in mankind. The government works on my behalf at times but not with delight. Our insurance companies may act for our good but not for the joy of it. My workplace may give benefits or represent me but not for the fun of it. But Wisdom *delights* in being the craftsman in my life.

It is no greater challenge to God to create harmony between my boss and myself than it was to secure the mountains. It is no greater puzzle for Him to match a woman's gifts and a spot in the workplace than it was to establish the clouds in their sphere. Setting boundaries in our relationships is not too great a challenge for the One who set boundaries for the turbulent sea.

The skeptic in me needs to see a drop of water or a lump of hardened lava to be reminded of the God who put Wisdom at my disposal to be my craftsman, Wisdom powerful enough to create my rock bowl. Dream world and practical, work world and play, the mundane, the eternal—all need to be offered to the craftsman, Wisdom, for engraving.

Lord, thank You
that You delight in my world—and in me, too.

16
Criticism

Do not rebuke a mocker or he will hate you; rebuke a wise man and he will love you. Instruct a wise man and he will be wiser still; teach a righteous man and he will add to his learning. (vv. 8-9)

Have you ever regarded a rebuke as an integral part of brotherly love? When God gave His laws to His people, He stated, "Rebuke your neighbor frankly" (Leviticus 19:17). Can you imagine a suburban town meeting with this bylaw? God gave that law for practical reasons. Confrontation reveals wrong, prevents hatred for the neighbor, and avoids complicity in the neighbor's sin or wrong behavior.

The law we prefer to quote instead is this: "Thou shall love your neighbor as yourself." But confrontation and rebuke are integrated with neighborly love in God's plan. Our individualistic, live-and-let-live society has separated the laws. We would rather file a piece of paper in a court than confront, discuss, and explain.

To rebuke is to render a judgment or to make a decision. Jacob wanted his neighbors to judge between Laban and himself when he had been accused. To rebuke is to hold a person accountable for his actions and blow the whistle on wrong behavior. Wrong actions between neighbors need not prevent love when rebuke and problem-solving are practiced.

51

What happens when you are rebuked at work? You may feel insecure, worried, hurt. But consider the positive. If your error had not been revealed, you would not change your behavior. Because you have been rebuked, you now have opportunity for learning, evaluation, and change. A mocker blames someone else. As long as we reject ownership of a mistake, we cannot take steps to correct it.

These verses in Proverbs show a progression: rebuke, instruct, teach. Rebuke renders a judgment. Instruction is the process of thinking through a complex arrangement resulting in wise dealing and use of common sense. Insight and comprehension describe instruction. Teaching involves more than comprehension. The Hebrew word means to know, to distinguish between good and evil. Revelation of the divine is included in teaching.

Christian working women want to know right from wrong, good from evil. Rebuke is often the first step and an integral part of that learning process. An action is judged. We then apply common sense by distinguishing good from evil. Recognizing that rebuke often comes before teaching helps me to readily accept it.

Perhaps you are in a position to rebuke someone. Maybe your job includes pointing out others' mistakes, Remembering that the law of rebuking should be accompanied by the law of neighborly love will moderate your tone of voice, your attitude, and your expectations.

In my work I deal with adolescents who are occasionally involved in substance abuse. Our policy is to confront the person rather than to ignore what he is doing, for ignoring the substance abuse enables the student to continue doing it. In the workplace at large we can profit from the same philosophy. Confronting rather than ignoring an issue can bring about a necessary change. When I am confronted, I can listen for instruction. In so doing, I can take a step toward fulfilling my calling as a righteous woman.

Lord, help me to love those who rebuke me.
I want to be a righteous woman.

17
Wise Choices

Stolen water is sweet; food eaten in secret is delicious. (v. 17)

Excitement throbbed through our young bodies. My heart pounded, my hands felt clammy. My sisters and I slipped barefoot behind the barn, a cigar in hand. We were going to experience the forbidden pleasures of adulthood.

Somehow we are all drawn to the stimulation of the "shouldn'ts": the child grasping the cookie or the cigar, the adolescent breaking curfew, the young adult violating a contract, the restless middle-ager breaking a marriage commitment. From the Garden of Eden to the present day, humans have not changed.

This chapter of Proverbs contrasts two women setting a table for others: the wise woman (vv. 1-6) and the foolish woman (vv. 13-18). We choose between the tables. The wise woman carefully prepares the meal: she marinates meat, mixes wine, sets the table. The scene shows anticipation, planning, and disciplined work. This hostess actively seeks and invites her guests.

The foolish woman simply calls out to whoever passes by. With no mention of preparation, she advertises thrills.

The meal prepared by the wise woman doesn't have the stimulation of the forbidden thrill, but it is satisfying for the long run. The meal prepared by the foolish woman looks more exciting temporarily, but those who partake of it pay their dues later. The one who eats the foolish woman's banquet enjoys the thrill but experiences the inner discomfort of knowing it is wrong. The cigar, the tainted money, the affair—all will bring inner discomfort, unless one's conscience has been hardened.

I recall the pain of my neighbor as he sat beside me in the bleachers watching a football game. He bounced his toddler son on one knee with his eyes glued to another son playing on the field, his son by a previous marriage. "I wouldn't have done it if I'd have known she would be so bitter, if I'd known how little I would see my kids."

It was not his weekend to "get" his teenager, so he sat high in the bleachers and watched and hurt. The beginning of the divorce was his affair. Now he had a new life, not exactly what he expected but what he had asked for by choosing the table at which he would sit.

Both women call "the simple." The Hebrew meaning of the term is "naive" or "immature." Ironically some of our foolish decisions and choices are based on our desire to appear mature. My sisters and I thought smoking would make us feel adult. But instead it made us nauseated, a far cry from independent freedom. Some thrills that beckon us lead to debt, robbery, immorality, the breaking of covenants, and even death. We may not actually murder someone, but in our pursuit of a thrill we can kill a relationship, extinguish innocence, or destroy our own credibility.

We need to listen wisely when we are called and examine the table before eating. We await a place prepared for us unmatched by any temporary thrill in this world.

Lord, change me
from a simple woman to Your wise daughter.

18
Finances

The wages of the righteous bring them life but the
income of the wicked brings them punishment.
(v. 16)

As women in the marketplace, we are faced with a new challenge our previous generation counterparts working in their homes did not face. We regularly get a paycheck, money in our name, presumably over which we control spending. All are not discretionary dollars, especially if you are a single parent. Most dollars should go two places, and you struggle to survive.

But for some, a paycheck offers more choices. Trump built glistening towers, though his marriage crumbled. Drexel Burnham Lambert, Inc., a privately owned firm specializing in junk bond financing, literally piled its goods on Wall Street when the firm collapsed three years after its peak. In 1986 its revenue was more than $5 billion and its profit more than $450. In 1989, Drexel filed for bankruptcy.

We may never have many dollars, but God has always been interested in how we spend what we have. And He cares about the little things: the one-talent steward, the sparrow, the widow with her mite. If we wisely carve out five dollars to help the poor, feed the hungry, provide shelter for the homeless, besides bringing life to someone else Proverbs says we bring life to ourselves. "Diligent hands bring wealth" (v. 4). Our responsibility is diligence; God's is wealth. He can and does multiply our resources, but we tie His hands by our sin and laziness.

Proverbs 11:26 advises us to provide for people's needs before investing for profit. First Timothy 5:8 reminds us that we should begin with the needs of our own family. "If anyone does not provide for his relatives, and especially for his immediate family, he has denied the faith and is worse than an unbeliever." Beyond family provision, we are told in 1 Timothy 6:18 to be rich in good deeds, generous, and willing to share.

As working women increasingly make dollar decisions, what difference will we make? Will we drive the market behind designer apparel and expensive recreational toys, or will we push back creeping hunger in Africa and promote better education for all our children, in ghettos and in comfortable suburbs? We contributed to the demise of the business suit with the miniskirt. Some women's apparel companies collapsed because of our vote with our dollar. Our spending choices are important.

On payday do you habitually open the envelope and study the numbers, as I do? The next time we go through that familiar ritual let us ask ourselves, *What could this income mean to God?* Proverbs 10:7 tells us, "The memory of the righteous will be a blessing, but the name of the wicked will rot."

The *Chicago Tribune*'s business section recently featured a picture of computers piled on the sidewalk of Wall Street. They were among the casualties of the collapse of a once mighty brokerage house that had made many enemies through its greed for wealth. On another page of the business section were pictures of the real estate jewels of the Trump empire. When these properties have crumbled and rusted, what memory will remain? If the glory went all to God, those memories will be sweet. But if glory was all for self-promotion, those memories will be rotten. Even a bowl of oatmeal for your child or a bowl of soup for the hungry can glorify God.

Lord, I give each dollar to You.
Direct my heart, mind, and wallet as I invest it.

19
Hatred

He who conceals his hatred has lying lips, and whoever spreads slander is a fool. (v. 18)

Hatred creates losers. You can't hide it inside. It pops out in what you say. If you say the right thing while hating the person, the positive things you say are lies. "I'm pleased for her promotion." "But surely she meant well." If you say what you feel, it's slander. "She didn't deserve it. Don't trust her." Whether our reasons for hatred are valid or not, we are foolish to hate. Hatred creates an indigestion that Rolaids cannot cure. Hatred stirs up old quarrels (Proverbs 10:12). Hatred sharpens our memory of what we should forget. We lose.

God approves hatred only when we hate what He hates: lying, scheming, false witnesses, shedding innocent blood, and violating His holiness. He does not keep His hatred secret. But He doesn't hate the person. He hates sin and what sin causes people to do. If I hate my co-worker or relative, I hate a person God created. Though we may sometimes hate sin in another person, more frequently we hate when someone hurts our pride or jars our shaky self-esteem.

I need to take my self-esteem to God so that He can transform it to God-esteem. I value myself because He made me. My success is due to His giving me strengths or blessing my weakness. He forgives and forgets my failures. With this foundation for God-esteem, we need not hate others for ill treatment of us.

Hate is erased by forgiveness. When we forgive we no longer need to hide our hatred and lie or express our hatred through slander. We give up our claim to compensation and absorb the injustice, bear the pain.

Forgiveness in the marketplace is uncommon. Personnel directors do not offer seminars on it, though forgiveness would probably improve the atmosphere. Can you imagine this poster: "Make IIB a better place to work: *Forgive.*" Our workplace may promote a mindset of "I must grasp what's mine" or "Equality must prevail from the bottom line dollar to the overtime minute." Christian working women can stand for equality and sometimes demand justice. But I pray that we do not lose the ability and willingness to forgive.

Forgiveness is based on what we believe about others and ourselves. The Bible teaches us two values about people. It teaches us that each of us is a miraculous creation of God—someone very special, and it teaches us that we are each depraved and sinful—worms. So we're all special worms. We're imperfect, inclined to be selfish, thoughtless, lazy, and even hateful. But we also have the capacity to be kind, giving, generous, productive, and loving. Your workplace is full of special worms, as is mine. Your friends and family are special worms, as are mine.

So we forgive and love, and we learn the meaning of Proverbs 10:12: "Hatred stirs up dissension, but love covers over all wrongs." We speak the truth in love (Ephesians 4:15). We do not flatter (false praise) because flattery is a form of hatred and wounds cruelly (Proverbs 26:28). We rejoice when another special worm is promoted. We praise her strengths and successes. We forgive when another special worm is rigid and cannot give us room to be ourselves. We forget her insult, forgive her error. We love what is special, while forgiving the worm.

Lord, help me to recognize hatred quickly so I can forgive. Give me respect for the special worms around me.

20
Getting Advice

For lack of guidance a nation falls, but many advisers make victory sure. (v. 14)

How accurate are your perceptions? I overestimate the total in my checkbook, underestimate my weight, and overestimate what my job evaluation will be. Students overestimate their grades, and Christians overestimate their morality while underestimating their sin.

By the time we reach adulthood we have accumulated a host of biases, blind spots, and emotional baggage. No wonder Proverbs advises us to seek counsel, listen to advisers, and respect what the previous generation has to say. To be an advice-seeker is not a revered role in our individualistic society. We admire the self-made man, the woman who has pulled herself up by her bootstraps, the person who's done it her way. Like the rich fool in Luke 12 who "thought to himself" and made a self-centered, self-destructive decision, we think we can make our decisions alone.

There are three distinct advantages to seeking counsel. Primarily we get more information. What individual alone has enough knowledge to lead a nation, a company, a church, a department, or a family? Strategic planning at work or for our personal goals requires information. Whether planning a strategy for selling, transportation, war, reaching a neighborhood, efficiency, or building character, we need information. We need advice from others whose experiences have been different from ours to check our biases. We need information from experts in areas different from ours. We need counsel from those who have touched a different side of the proverbial elephant.

I need advice for accountability. My decisions made in secret can be denied, avoided, postponed. To make a decision in secret is to say that we want no input from anyone else. In war, this may be wise. One does not want input from the enemy as to the best moment to attack. However, most of our decisions are better for having been informed by the perspective of others. Those who have given us input then are able to observe what we do with their advice. A sense of accountability is built up.

Groups such as Alcoholics Anonymous and Weight Watchers have relied on the principle of accountability as a change agent. Often a prayer group provides spiritual accountability. Verbalizing a problem is a beginning, but reporting the results of prayer gives us still more strength. A businessman asked my husband to hold him accountable when he was tempted to be unfaithful. We can ask a trusted friend to hold us accountable in a challenging work relationship.

There is a third benefit in seeking advice from others: it is humbling. When I ask my counseling mentor for input, she sees my lack of skill. When my husband and I ask for ideas from other parents, they see our inadequacies. We are found not to have all the answers. We admit we are human.

To ask a question is to publicize our weakness or ignorance. The edges of our pride curl, our stiff neck bends, and our shoulders stoop—good exercises for each of us. If we possessed all the answers, we wouldn't need others and we wouldn't need God. The world needs only one ultimate Source of all information. The rest of us were created to depend on each other and on Him.

Lord, help me to listen to wise advisers.
Help me find an accountability partner.

21
Paradox Giving

One man gives freely, yet gains even more; another withholds unduly, but comes to poverty. A generous man will prosper; he who refreshes others will himself be refreshed. (vv. 24-25)

There are many paradoxes in Scripture. If you give, you become rich. If you refresh others, you become refreshed. Loving others increases the love you have within yourself. Much of what is truly real cannot be seen. Serving is true living.

It is no wonder that people reject Christianity. It just doesn't gel with our worldly way of thinking. We think that if we want, we must take; that if we need refreshment, we must hibernate in a health spa; that if we give love, we will be hurt or depleted. We believe what we see and feel. These messages come from business journals, commercials, advertisements, and self-help publications. No wonder we stumble at the cross.

"Do not conform any longer to the pattern of this world, but be transformed by the renewing of your mind" (Romans 12:2a). In order to live the paradoxes of Christianity I have to be transformed daily with a different mind-set. What does it mean to be transformed in your workplace? I don't know your space, but I can tell you about mine. To be transformed is to ask with genuine interest about the welfare of co-workers, to refill the empty coffee pot when someone else took the last cup, to pedal without complaining when a blunder requires extra effort on the part of all, to carefully phrase a response when one disagrees with a decision.

If I could be transformed to that meager extent, I would be *living* at work, not just putting in time. How else might I be transformed? By complimenting others more frequently, especially that co-worker who grates on me. By being content when my extra effort goes unnoticed. By investing extra care in a student whose parent will never write a commendation letter. Your workplace is different from mine, but you can imagine transformations. Visualize specifically how you could refresh someone at work.

When we live transformed lives in our workplace, another paradox occurs. The person who would not approach the cross because Christianity seems so absurd will look again at this curious way of living that brings satisfaction when there is no glory, contentment when there is no raise, joy when the world is not amusing.

"He who wins souls is wise" (Proverbs 11:30). Whether our witness is silent or spoken, we are wise to bring others to God. This is another paradox. When we give away our faith and reveal God through our transformed behavior, instead of having less, we have more. We approach God again, this time with a new person beside us, and we see Him in a new way. We see how uniquely He works in each person's life. Instead of taking out of our small basket of faith for another, depleting our basket, we find our basket full again, our faith increasing.

Remember Jesus' commendation of the widow who gave two mites (Luke 21:1-4)? His criterion was willingness and sacrifice, not quantity. We need to look at what we have and be generous at what we can do and do it willingly. After we have acted, we will experience the paradox. "Then you will be able to test and approve what God's will is—his good, pleasing and perfect will" (Romans 12:2*b*). The absurd paradox need not be explained. Its proof is in the living.

Lord, help me be Your paradox where I work.

22
Imitations

*Better to be a nobody and yet have a servant
than pretend to be somebody and have no food.
(v. 9)*

Is it real? The fifteen dollar Gucci purse at the flea
market is not. The inexpensive diamond in the window
may be a cubic zirconium. The mushrooming designer
clothing industry was rapidly followed by imitations,
from jeans to bed linens, dishes, and perfumes. Where
there is growing business, there is customer demand.
And customer demand stems from the human heart.
We often want to look like what we are not, we want
others to perceive us as we wish to be, not who we really are.

God is interested in the real person inside. He
knows what is real and what is imitation. "Man looks
at the outward appearance, but the Lord looks at the
heart" (1 Samuel 16:7). He knows our real needs as
well as what we think we need. God knows about the
rent and the grocery bills. He knows who is depending
on us.

An important Proverbs principle is that we first
earn and then spend. "Finish your outdoor work and
get your fields ready; and after that, build your house"
(24:27). We work first and then decide how we shall
live. Our society tells us to decide what we want and

how we prefer to live, and then to borrow or charge it if we haven't earned it. The Proverbs principle tells us that it is better to be a nobody with security (having a servant or slave symbolized being able to provide comfortably for your household) than to be a somebody without security.

When we live by the Proverbs principle, we will have the inner security of knowing that we are not financially overextended. It is a quiet peace, a feeling different from the thrill of wearing new clothes. Unquestionably, new things can give a temporary lift, which is not wrong, provided we can afford what we have. The danger is when we need the outer splash for inner security.

One advertisement for women's hair color says, "It costs more, but I'm worth it." Another says, "You owe it to yourself." Appealing to our need for self-love, the advertisement implies that we need to spend on ourselves to prove we love ourselves. When we can't afford the splash, we feel less lovable.

It just doesn't work. Getting hooked on a superficial feeling of security tempts us to pretend to be a somebody, to spend what we have not earned to keep up external appearances.

We are *God's* somebody. Chosen by Him (Ephesians 1:4), enjoyed by Him (Ephesians 1:5), planned for by Him (Psalm 139:16), prepared by Him for the future (John 14:2). We are gifted (Romans 12:6), strengthened (Colossians 1:11), and empowered (Colossians 1:11). With this identity as daughters of God, who needs to pretend?

Lord, I'd rather be Yours and be nobody to the world than to be the universe's most famous woman without You.

23
Speech

A fool shows his annoyance at once, but a prudent man overlooks an insult. . . . A prudent man keeps his knowledge to himself, but the heart of fools blurts out folly. (vv. 16, 23)

I was arguing with my boss. Our chief exercise was jumping on the end of each other's sentences. I later reflected on that conversation and reread this portion of Proverbs. Solomon's wisdom impressed me. Words spoken so many years ago proved to be relevant again in my world.

Look at the power and effect of words.

1. We can be trapped by saying the wrong thing (v. 13).
2. We can feel satisfaction just as physical labor brings satisfaction and rewards (v. 14).
3. We can listen and avoid mistakes (v. 15).
4. We can display our annoyance (v. 16).
5. We can give honest testimony (v. 17).
6. We can bring healing to others and ourselves (v. 18).
7. We can say something valuable for the long run (v. 19).
8. We can reveal our inner deceit (v. 20).
9. We can promote peace (v. 20).
10. We can dig our trouble hole deeper (v. 21).
11. We can bring delight to God (v. 22).
12. We can spread ignorance (v. 23).
13. We can cheer anxious people (v. 25).

In my mind's ear, our argument sounded like Dvor-ák's *New World Symphony*. This moving, adrenalin-producing work is punctuated by what has been called a *grand pause*. Would that I more frequently inserted a grand pause into my discussions. In music its purpose is to allow the last movement to be heard fully, to focus the senses on what is coming next. I need such a pause in my conversations, especially the tense ones. In that silence I can remember what I know to be true, can consider what has happened. I can reflect on what has been said, can consider where the conversation is going, can assess the consequences of my words. The grand pause draws attention to what is taking place. It can cover an insult and provide space for knowledge to reenter. It can be an exercise in self-control. It can change retort to response, hardening to hearing, disaster to positive dynamic.

I needed a grand pause with God, a set-apart time to pray and fast and listen for God's wisdom. During my commuting time, I made a list of how I could use my tongue for good. I could write commendations to students who seldom received recognition and were showing improvement. I could praise a secretary who pleasantly fulfills my typing needs. I could call a parent whose son was testing her patience and report a positive incident involving him. My list grew. When I reached the parking lot, I raced into the office, so anxious to begin executing my positive tongue list that I left the headlights on.

Perhaps your tongue will always be your challenge. I understand. "For out of the overflow of his heart his mouth speaks" (Luke 6:45). In our grand pause with God we can ask Him to change our hearts. In time our words as well will be affected.

Lord, give me a heart
that will overflow with good things.

24
Heroes

The light of the righteous shines brightly, but the lamp of the wicked is snuffed out. (v. 9)

Who are your heroes? What do you admire in them? I am deeply moved standing before the Lincoln Monument in Washington, D.C. Though its size and design are impressive, the philosophy Lincoln stood for is more awe-inspiring than the monument. With willingness to accept the hatred of those who disagreed with him, he took his stand, speaking boldly of the the blood slaves had shed in silence. Others have been more eloquent than Lincoln; others have accumulated more wealth. But in few has the light of justice shown more brightly than in Lincoln.

We read letters left for us by the apostles Paul, Peter, James, and John. Those letters inspire us and redirect our tongues, our hands, and our checkbooks. Judas, however, left no letters. He left no light for our daily living.

Nations have philosophical heroes. Those heroes are remembered as long as their ideas work. Witness the change in who is revered in Russia today. Companies remind new employees of founders, past presidents, and chairmen who have left a positive legacy, spelled p-r-o-f-i-t. I ask myself, *Who is lighting my path today? Whom do I admire?*

The light of Abigail's righteousness shines on my path. First Samuel 25 describes her life-changing crisis. She was married to a hard-drinking, ignorant fool. Yet she did not languish, fretting over what might have been. Her household respected her, she knew the political situation in her area, and her faith was strong. She was able to respond to crisis with a cool head, a wise assessment of the spiritual implications of the problem, and an organized effort toward its resolution.

Abigail rapidly assembled an enormous care package to cool David's anger. Her example of industry, initiating action, and practical decision-making is an admirable example for working women. But the righteousness that made her a light in the dark is demonstrated in this statement: "Please forgive your servant's offense, for the Lord will certainly make a lasting dynasty for my master, because he fights the Lord's battles . . . the life of my master will be bound securely in the bundle of the living by the Lord your God" (vv. 28a, 29b). She recognized that though her husband was a wealthy landowner with flocks of thousands and David a roving scavenger without job or home, Nabal was the servant and David the master.

When Abigail later told Nabal what she had done, "his heart died within him so that he became as a stone" (v. 37). He died ten days later. What a graphic illustration of the lamp of the wicked being snuffed out.

God does not always work so rapidly. Sometimes future generations are the first to see the difference between the light of the righteous and the lamp of the wicked. Some will be revealed only at the time of judgment. Meanwhile, God has given me sufficient examples from whom to choose the heroes who light my world.

Lord, help me choose my heroes
and provide righteous light for others.

25
People Prints

He who walks with the wise grows wise, but a
companion of fools suffers harm. (v. 20)

Most humans are covered with people prints. We
bear the marks of all who have touched our lives. Some
people prints have major impact; others leave barely
discernable impressions. We admit the undeniable
DNA imprint that determines physical characteristics
and on which paternity suits can be based. We less readily own that people prints are mental and emotional
and spiritual.

Look at the variety of people prints in Proverbs:
the call of the prostitute, the light of the righteous, the
instruction of parents. Proverbs frequently speaks of
how others shape us. This proverb says that we should
walk with the wise if wisdom is our goal.

Why not just sit at the feet of the wise and listen to
their lectures? Perhaps because wisdom is not inter-
nalized until we see it in action. I observed a well-
known woman in a crowd of admirers. People were
pressing for her attention, waiting their turn. A teenager, jean-clad with tousled hair, pressed through. The
woman immediately attended to his questions while
the others waited. He was her son, and she treated him
as the most important person in the crowd. Later she
said to me, "Most people you know, including your co-

workers, will hardly remember your name in ten years. In twenty-five years your relationship with your children will be the product of today." I remembered her words because I had walked beside her and had observed what she meant.

Wisdom is not tested in the classroom. Its proof is on the streets, in the pits, at the desk, in the hallways, at the family roundtable. We become wiser by watching wise people in action.

Psalms tells us we will be blessed by avoiding wicked people. "Blessed is the man who does not walk in the counsel of the wicked or stand in the way of sinners or sit in the seat of mockers" (Psalm 1:1). The progression of sin is clearly outlined. First we move alongside the wrong person. Maybe it is unavoidable that we be near her, for we work together. Maybe we are getting acquainted, being sociable. But then we stand there. We assume a fixed position. We are either comfortable with who she is or we are stimulated by our interaction with her. We may stay because of attraction or because of circumstances. Then we sit beside her. We become her companion. We're one of the gang. We're in.

We're in *trouble.* We're temporarily imprinted at best, impacted for a lifetime at worst. If we must work with someone who has a negative influence on us, we must counterbalance that influence by a wise person's impact. A person or small group can be our source of accountability. I will always be a sinner—"prone to wander, Lord I feel it." Though I've been a Christian for twenty-three years, sometimes the council of the wicked still sounds good to me. But it is selfish, self-promoting, ego-boosting, and worthless for eternity.

Time and distance can be our tools for wisdom. To the extent possible, we can minimize negative contacts or keep them confined to a space and time in which we can maintain our Christian covenant. When we are weak, overstressed, or spiritually depleted, we need to be especially careful of where we walk. We had little control over the people prints of our childhood, but we are adults now. Our paths and our companions are now our own choosing.

Lord, may the greatest people print on me
be made by Jesus Christ.

26
Home

The wise woman builds her house, but with her own hands the foolish one tears hers down. . . . The house of the wicked will be destroyed, but the tent of the upright will flourish. (vv. 1, 11)

House means wood and brick today. In Solomon's day the meaning included family and household. We invest much work and money to protect our dwellings from outside destruction. We caulk crumbling mortar, insulate so that water pipes won't freeze, and paint to protect wood. We take precautions to protect our families such as buying life insurance, investigating and selecting schools for our children's education, and choosing neighborhoods that we hope are safe.

Most families, however, aren't destroyed by external crises; they crumble from within.

No woman purposefully goes about destroying her family. Destruction usually begins subtly like dry rot in wood. Training becomes tyranting where children feel unknown and unloved. Correction becomes exasperation when parents lose patience. Protection becomes prison because we can't let go for the young adult to become accountable. Worrying becomes enmeshment because we can't separate others' responsibilities from our own. Building a healthy house is especially difficult these days.

How can a wise woman build her house? What do we need at home? Children, especially adolescents, need many things from their home.

Home needs to be a safe place where one is secure and unharmed. Home needs to be an unsafe place where there are unknowns to be mastered. Home needs reasonable controls so that physical needs, such as sleep and nourishment, are satisfied. Home needs the absence of some controls so that one can experiment with making decisions and learning accountability.

Home should contain people who know and love us. That's part of security. Sometimes people who don't know and love us can help us appreciate what we have. No wonder home building is a challenge! There are so many contradictions.

Proverbs provides encouragement. Even a tent can flourish. Canvas that occasionally leaks rain and a floor soaked with rainwater can dry with rearranging and time. Pegs can be moved if strong winds loosen them. The door can be pinned back if it's stuffy. A tent has flexibility, which every household needs. We are clans of different people, different temperaments, varying motivations. Bedrooms for bodies is not as important as room for differences. We may not be able to avoid illnesses, unemployment, accidents, or even death. But we can secure our canvas in a new shape to protect our redefined family.

Proverbs's contrast of houses and tents reminds us that all is not what is seen on the outside. The house may look permanent, but it can crumble. A tent may appear fragile, but it can endure. All houses will eventually crumble or go up in smoke, but people are eternal. I observed a baby in a hospital intensive care nursery. His tiny, pumping legs were the size of a short pencil. I wondered if he weighed even two pounds. But he was more valuable than the thousands of dollars' worth of monitors surrounding him and the millions of dollars' worth of construction in the already huge but expanding health complex in which his little bed lay.

The temporary was the brick and mortar, steel beams, and construction housing the seemingly unstoppable equipment. The eternal was the tiny bit of flesh created in God's image.

Lord, help me to build up
the people in my household with love
and to use my house or tent for Your glory.

27
National Wealth

The wealth of the wise is their crown, but the fol-
ly of fools yields folly. . . . Righteousness exalts
a nation, but sin is a disgrace to any people. (vv.
24, 34)

Wealth earned by work seems old-fashioned these days. Speculation sounds more sophisticated—until you read the newspapers. As taxpayers we will "supplement" speculation to the tune of 5 billion dollars to minimize the disaster of the savings and loan fiasco. When restrictions on borrowing money for speculation were eased, speculators started to build hotels where there were no tourists and apartment buildings where there were few renters. Speculators built anything that would gain them access to investment dollars.

They hadn't done their homework. Complexes had to be left unfinished. Market value turned out to be smaller than the money borrowed. Bankruptcy followed. Now all of us who faithfully pay our mortgages are paying.

Proverbs calls wise wealth a crown. What is wise wealth? "All hard work brings a profit" (v. 23a). "Honest scales and balances are from the Lord; all the weights in the bag are of his making" (16:11). In the field of real estate we might substitute the "appraisal" for "scale." "Be sure you know the condition of your flocks, give careful attention to your herds" (27:23).

"Buy the truth and do not sell it; get wisdom, discipline and understanding" (23:23).

Wise wealth begins with knowing what you have, then tending it for growth. Today we tend a company, a building, or a catering service instead of herds. Whether our wealth consists of concrete or livestock or the inventory of a boutique, supervision may be a part of our work. Wise wealth recognizes God as the giver of increases. The rich and poor are given sight by God (29:13). He sends the sunshine and rain.

You may be the decision-maker in accumulating wealth, or you may be one of many employees, a cog in a large wheel. In either position you can bring glory to God by your work. "Like the coolness of snow at harvest time is a trustworthy messenger to those who send him; he refreshes the spirit of his masters" (25:13). A trustworthy employee is as refreshing as a spring rain.

Did you know that your work exalts our nation? What you and I produce determines the quality and quantity of the services and products of our nation. Many indices measure these elements and compare them to other countries. The value of the dollar, fluctuating interest rates, the Gross National Product—all depend on our work. When we work with honest scales, when we carry out our jobs knowledgeably and prudently, we exalt our nation.

Major sources of profit loss in our country include employee theft and lowered productivity or error due to substance abuse. These economic problems begin with sin or the effects of sin on ravaged families and individuals. If we were a nation of righteous employees, our nation would profit. Though profit should not be our primary motive, God can be honored by wise wealth. Christian working women can exalt our nation by living out Christian ethics where they work.

Lord, help me to be a righteous employee
because I love You.

28
Contentment

*Better a little with the fear of the Lord than great
wealth with turmoil. (v. 16)*

Contentment: elusive, temporary, evasive, tenta-
tive. We all wish for it but never place it on our New
Year's resolution list. We want a better job, fewer
pounds, the ideal family, professional commendation,
individual recognition, a raise, more perks, a new look.
Sometimes in our quiet life-probing moments we pon-
der what life would be like if we had all our wishes.

I would probably just move my sights higher if I
achieved my goals today. What professional challenge
could I tackle next? Another degree? Getting skinny
would mean I'd have more wrinkles that would need
removing. My human heart is never satisfied.

Proverbs tells me that less is more. Little with the
Lord is more than I need. All I could ever wish for
would be more than I could manage without the Lord.
"All the days of the oppressed are wretched, but the
cheerful heart has a continual feast" (v. 15). When we
gloomily think of what we want but don't have, contentment cannot penetrate our emotions. When contentment births a cheerful heart, what little we have
seems sufficient.

Our family occasionally spends a week in the only
cabin on an island. We don't worry about the lawn

82

mower's breaking because the "lawn" is pine needles on sparse grass. The shower can't leak because it is a garden hose tied to an outside tree. The garbage disposal can't jam, and the air conditioner can't malfunction. Simple and primitive, our week is full of contentment. We feast on watching the eagle's nest across the bay, or counting the duck families that come for corn. We drink in rainbow sunsets that turn from pastel blue to peach to mauve to subtle red orange and deep purple. "Little" is almost more than our senses can absorb. The contentment we find there is not what we've brought to the island. Little is much; the simple life is profoundly rich.

How does one achieve contentment? Can we make a list? Step one, step two. Check. Check. Finally one reaches the goal? I think not. Contentment overtakes us in our pursuit of being Christlike. Loving God, learning God, opening our human hearts for Him to change, in the midst of our walking, tripping, stumbling, contentment emerges unexpectedly. Comforting a troubled co-worker, listening to a child, deciding to smooth a rocky relationship, not giving up on a testing teenager, encouraging a tired volunteer—then contentment overtakes me.

Stretching out our tired bodies at the end of the day can simply be sign-off time. But lying down with reverence for the Lord, with a sense that at least some of our day was different because we love God, is not just signing off. It's ending the day with contentment. Maybe you are not another notch higher on the professional ladder. Maybe there has been no bonus, no trophy, no commendation. But godliness with contentment is great gain (1 Timothy 6:6).

Lord, thank You for Your constant acceptance,
consistent love, and permanent forgiveness.
What a feast!

29
Humility

The fear of the Lord teaches a man wisdom, and
humility comes before honor. (v. 33)

The word *humility* is a seldom used today. In my
position I frequently complete recommendations for
people. Some have checklists of desirable qualities on
which I am to rate the individual. But I have never seen
humility on the list. My Hebrew dictionary tells me it is
learned in the school of affliction. No wonder we don't
want that characteristic; it is learned in the least appreciated school! But honor means glory, and that has
a nice ring to it. If humility is part of the process on the
way to glory, let's at least investigate it.

If you are in one of those ragged seasons, stages
that you hope will pass quickly, tough times, you may
graduate a humble person. Why do we learn humility
in tough times? Because we don't need a deliverer
when we can deliver ourselves. When we can't make it
on our own, we see God as our Deliverer. "He guides
the humble in what is right and teaches them his way"
(Psalm 25:9). In our school of affliction, most of us are
more teachable. And when we are teachable, a teacher
appears. We learn something that the successful, always self-sufficient person never learns: that God can
carry us through any difficulty, any season, any crisis.
A humble person knows God the Deliverer.

The school of affliction also shows us God the Provider. When we cannot clearly decide what to do next, when we must step into the unknown, we learn how faith feels. When our wisdom is useless and we can plan no more, we meet God the Provider. He keeps the widow's boundaries intact but tears down the boundaries of the proud (v. 25). He cares for us when we can do nothing for ourselves.

We think of honor going to the strong, of glory belonging to conquerors. But honor is another of Proverbs's paradoxes. When we are powerless to solve our own problems, we become humble; and humility comes before honor. The powerless woman can become a woman of great honor. Paul asks us in Romans whether trouble or hardship or any humiliating experience will separate us from God. "No, in all these things we are more than conquerors through him who loved us" (8:37).

Surely Jesus' most humiliating moment was when He hung on the cross, naked, a failure by every criteria His followers had established. But in that moment of humility, dying, He unleashed God's power to give Him life again, a greater victory than any of His followers were expecting.

What moments of humility do you fear? A child's dropping out of school? Being abandoned by a friend? Losing your job? Not getting a promotion? Your teenager's running away? Losing your wallet? Some crises seem large, others small. At the moment, size is determined by our perspective, not necessarily reality. You and I can become women of honor in our powerless moments by accepting the teacher of affliction. Remember, humility comes before honor.

Times of trouble bring us more closely in touch with God's love—and what greater honor can we have than the love of God?

Lord, help me learn quickly.

30
Peace

When a [woman's] ways are pleasing to the Lord, he makes even [her] enemies live at peace with [her]. (v. 7)

"Blessed are the peacemakers, for they will be called sons of God" (Matthew 5:9). Perhaps no other characteristic, besides love, so identifies a person as a Christian as that of being a peacemaker.

A worldly person can be generous because it is tax deductible. One can show mercy in order to look good to others. Kindness might motivate a returned favor. But what is to be gained from being a peacemaker? Marketplaces, homes, and even churches often do not recognize this ability.

Being a peacemaker pleases God, and He rewards this rare characteristic with a gift no one else can give. He brings more peace.

Have you ever noticed how hard it is to be angry at a co-worker who is a peacemaker? Have you noticed that you cannot even envy her. Let me describe a woman I admire who is a peacemaker.

She is humble. She is not self-promoting.

She gives a day's work for a day's wages.

She pulls her weight on the team. When things are done well, she shares the credit with the whole team.

She is fair. She is ethical and trustworthy.

She doesn't put others down through gossip, insult, or innuendo. She expects the best of the rest of us, not the worst.

This woman is a nonprovoking lady. No wonder others live at peace with her. The characteristics she possesses are godly. The closer I come to living as a godly woman, the more of a peacemaker I'll be.

Proverbs 16:28 tells us that a perverse person stirs up dissension, and a gossip separates close friends. Perverse means to twist or turn. Our human heart sometimes wants to twist information to be attention-getting or to turn facts so that they make us look good. Isn't this often what destroys peace in your workplace? We can work contentedly with others when they are promoted, popular, and precocious—unless they achieve those things by twisting facts at others' expense.

When we are Christlike we don't have to think, "What should I do to be a peacemaker today?" If we are humble and fair in our workplace, peace will be a by-product.

No matter what you do or how you live, there may be individuals who will not share peace with you. I appreciate Paul's encouragement: "If it is possible, as far as it depends on you, live at peace with everyone" (Romans 12:18). He had just advised us never to repay evil for evil and to strive always to do what is right in the eyes of everybody. Yet he recognized that we can't please 'em all. "If it is possible . . ."

Abraham Lincoln in his second inaugural address illustrated the heart of the peacemaker, even though all were not at peace with him. "With malice toward none; with charity for all, with firmness in the right as God gives us to see the right," he said. When we work with that heart attitude, we can say, "Lord to the extent possible, for the part that depends on me, I want to live at peace with everyone."

Lord, help me live as You did.

31
Power

The lot is cast into the lap, but its every decision is from the Lord. (v. 33)

Enhance your impact. Learn the verbal and nonverbal behaviors among women that are perceived as either diminishing or enhancing personal power. Learn how to create a powerful first impression and orchestrate it all—the words, the voice, the behavior. Be an impressive package!

Now there's a seminar I should attend. People would listen to me, think I was a put-together woman, and be impressed. My self-esteem would rise, my confidence grow. Maybe I would even make better decisions.

Are you ever drawn to voices that promise you they can teach you to be more impressive, more powerful? I am. It's an attractive thought to imagine people waiting on me for my decisions. Surely the world awaits the transformed me.

Proverbs says that the lot is cast into the lap, but its every decision is from the Lord. Doesn't this seem like an unsophisticated way to decide things? In our age of policy manuals, complex legal systems, information gathering, free enterprise, juries, panels, and experts, the casting of lots hardly sounds like a reliable resource. But as a student of Proverbs, I need to remember that God is in control.

In Old Testament times property ownership, the dividing up of the spoils of war, and sometimes life and death were determined by how a few pebbles fell in the lap. The whole future of a tribe might be set by those few stones.

I should not be surprised. Is it any more difficult for God to control the fall of a few pebbles than a human heart, a person's mind, or the vote of a jury?

Proverbs gives godly advice on how to get things done. "Better a patient man than a warrior, a man who controls his temper than one who takes a city" (v. 32). I observed a godly broadcaster move the Federal Communication Commission by patience and prayer. Storming a citadel may not open doors like the power of patient persistence.

Using worldly techniques and schemes to accomplish goals results in pride when we take credit for the outcome. We admire the results of our projections, our research, our power plays. We did it ourselves. Verse 18 tells us that pride precedes a fall. Though we must function within this world's systems, it is God who controls results. If our efforts fail, we must go to God for further wisdom, perhaps for forgiveness, and increase our trust in Him. If the results of our labors are positive, we humbly thank God, good stumbling insurance.

I am encouraged by God's standard of excellence for me. He simply wants me to be faithful (1 Corinthians 4:4). When I look at this criterion, I can trust the events in my work to impact decisions in my life as He chooses. Being an "impressive package" is not His objective for me. But seeing that I trust Him for every decision is.

Lord, help me in every area of my life
to cast my lot with You.

32
Sensitivity

*The crucible for silver and the furnace for gold,
but the Lord tests the heart. . . . A rebuke im-
presses a man of discernment more than a hun-
dred lashes a fool. (vv. 3, 10)*

I met with a frustrated, sensitive administrator today. He is one of those rare individuals who, in spite of
the number of reports he has to generate, volume of
work, sometimes unfair procedures related to his position, has not lost his heart. You know what I mean,
don't you? Some people forget that they are dust as
they move up the ladder. But not this man.

Work can change us, however. We may find ourselves in circumstances where it is more feasible to lie
than to be truthful, more popular to quote policy than
to act in the best interests of people, to repeat a matter
that should remain quiet for reasons of our own prosperity. In other words, work can squeeze our hearts.
We can become callous women.

Wouldn't it be wonderful if, as women fill more
and higher positions in the work force, more "heart"
were brought to the factory, the public school, the hospital, the company?

God tests our hearts. He gives us challenges in the
form of opportunity to choose what is fair and kind.
Goods and services are temporary, but people aren't.

God gives us tests to see if we live by His policy regarding the importance and dignity of people. He gives us opportunity to be sensitive to others.

Being sensitive to others can be painful. You feel another's pain or despair. You want to change things that are unfair even when it is beyond your power to do so. You *feel*. You feel when you are criticized. A fool can be beaten with no impact; but if you are sensitive, a word of rebuke is enough for you to get the message.

Sometimes when we have experienced the pain of sensitivity, we want to bury our heart somewhere down inside so that it is untouchable by injustice or personal pain. How is your heart? Let's not forget that we are dust—the kind of dust that can turn to stone under the stresses of life and pressures of work.

When tests come, we can say, "Lord, is this a heart test? I don't want to need pounding in a crucible or melting down in a fire for You to refine me. I want to respond to Your rebuke. I don't want to be so insensitive I can only be reached through lashes."

Jesus wept with those who wept, felt compassion for the hungry masses, was tender to the humiliated sinner. We can maintain a sensitive heart in a competitive world only if we keep close to Jesus.

Lord, test my heart to keep it pure.
Help the fires in my workplace to remove my impurities
so that I will be like You.

33
Justice

*Acquitting the guilty and condemning the inno-
cent, the Lord detests them both. . . . It is not
good to punish an innocent man, or to flog officials for their integrity. (vv. 15, 26)*

In my work environment, there is a big emphasis
on "doing things right." As a counselor in a public
high school, I push lots of paper. We have a manual
that weighs seven and one-quarter pounds. If I don't
do things right, I may end up scheduling students for
the wrong classes, encouraging them to take the
wrong programs, counseling them toward inappropriate future plans.

One of the dangers of concentrating on "doing
things right" is that you can become so preoccupied
with detail that you don't do the right *thing.* We hear of
cases where the guilty go free on technicalities. Sometimes the innocent are caught in the net intended for
the guilty. Not only is our world complicated, sometimes it is simply unfair. I need to ask myself frequently,
Am I doing the right thing? Am I serving the student
by this action? Have the policies drowned people?

If our laws penalize the innocent and punish the
good, we need to change the laws. True, it is easier
sometimes to say, "I'm just doing my job." But 1 Corinthians 4:4 tells me that I am to be a faithful servant.

My workplace is an arena of servanthood. Christian working women are to be salt in the marketplace, a light wherever they work. They are to be faithful wherever they are. God asks them to "do the right thing" in every sphere of their lives.

Sometimes we think naively that justice will automatically prevail. That will only be true in eternity. By definition justice is conforming to spiritual law. Our country has been blessed by the benefits of the Judeo-Christian ethic, which is our foundation for justice. But that ethic is eroding. We commonly quote crime statistics to prove this, yet I think white collar greed saddens God's heart just as much, and seems to be increasing even faster than violence. Sometimes the guilty are promoted, the innocent fired, the fair official passed over for promotion, and the bribe taker moved up the ladder.

Perverting justice costs countless dollars, hardens hearts, and discourages employees from giving an honest day's work for an honest day's pay. But there is an even more tragic cost. The heart of the wicked is increasingly hardened each time she perverts the course of justice. Eventually she can callously wipe her mouth and say, "I've done nothing wrong" (30:20).

Pontius Pilate washed his hands and said, "I am innocent. It's not my problem" (Matthew 27:24). But washing his hands did not purify his heart, and denying his accountability did not remove his name from the eternal record of participants in our Lord's crucifixion. Scripture gives us many examples of people who meant well but perverted justice.

Doing things right is a laudable goal, but it is not as laudable as doing the right thing. We need to keep clear communication with our just God, who knows not only our actions but our motivations.

Lord, help me to promote justice.

34
The Work Ethic

One who is slack in his work is brother to one who destroys. (v. 9)

Workaholics, lazy people, overachievers, nonperformers—there are all kinds of workers. Christians hear many messages about doing their best, working as unto the Lord, doing whatever they do with all their might. Paul told the idle people in Thessalonica to settle down and earn the bread they ate (2 Thessalonians 3:11-13). Jesus told His listeners to render unto Caesar the things that were Caesar's.

I need to be reminded of these truths. Many of us fear starting a new project or hesitate to implement a new idea or program because we will have to pedal faster to fit it into our responsibilities. Like it or not, many will evaluate our Christianity by our work in the marketplace.

Some of us are also mothers or family facilitators. As a working parent, I am tempted sometimes to give my best at work and the leftovers to my family. My children are reasonably accepting of leftover food, but I can do real damage by trying to nourish their spirits with leftover, depleted emotions.

We must constantly assess and balance where and how we work, where and how we invest our energy, emotions, and patience. In our culture, "work" means the marketplace. But the biblical concept is broader. Work is subduing the earth in the marketplace, at home, in the government. Those areas were intended to be integrated and balanced in God's plan for His people. In our nation they are often fragmented; working for one may mean working against another. Working women are often caught in this opposition. The marketplace may never support positive policies for our families, though some successful companies are moving in that direction.

It seems to me that we women must daily, even hourly, make difficult decisions about our work. We want to give what we can and what is fair to our workplace, but we must also work for the good of our families.

We cannot be slack in our work, but we must balance the marketplace work ethic with our need to devote time and energy to our other covenants. Like a well, we cannot supply all buckets. We will dry out if we indiscriminately ladle ourselves into the marketplace, our children, our mate, our aging parents. When that happens something will have to be sacrificed. It may be a relationship, communication with a teenager, or our enthusiasm for the coming day.

As I evaluate my work, I frequently ask myself, What will be important ten years from now? What covenants have I made? What commitments are already in place? I lay these before the Lord. Sometimes I say, "Lord, my well is empty. Help me prioritize my work. What are Your priorities for these covenants?" He shows me what is Caesar's and what is His, and often after our time together, I discover my well is full again.

Lord, may my daily life
win the respect of others for Your glory
as I balance my covenant relationships.

35
Listening

The first to present his case seems right, till another comes forward and questions him. (v. 17)

Have you ever been part of a jury? What a learning experience! I listened as one person questioned a witness. I began to form an opinion. When the same witness was questioned by a different person, entirely different information was revealed and my opinion shifted.

No wonder Proverbs advises us to listen before we speak. The wise woman listens patiently. Frequently her first words are questions, not answers. Earlier we examined the complexity of the world in which we live and work. Information helps us make rational decisions and sound judgments, not just in the marketplace, but in every sphere of life. "A fool finds no pleasure in understanding but delights in airing his own opinions" (18:2). Usually if my mouth is engaged, my ears are blocked. Taking in information and processing it is difficult when we are talking.

As the parent of four children I am challenged daily to make decisions regarding their disputes. Who is right? What is fair? I have learned the truth of Proverbs 18:13, "He who answers before listening—that is his folly and his shame." I have let justice roll down after hearing only one side. Then, when more information surfaced, I have found that I acted too quickly and without full understanding. Those stories surface later to my shame. "Remember when Mom . . ?" And the story is told of my speedy attempt at justice.

The value of listening to both sides is profitable in the workplace. One person may not purposely color the facts, but we each do see life through one set of eyes. Listening gives me another set of eyes. I can subject my perspective to another's insights. Nearsightedness is balanced by listening to possible long-range impact. Farsightedness is balanced by seeing current effects of an action.

Sometimes even after all our listening and questioning, we cannot make a firm decision. Some issues are like sibling rivalry—either decision, you leave one child staring sulkingly. Verse 18 offers a solution. Cast lots or draw straws. When both consequences of a decision are similar, this procedure may be a wise solution. Strong opponents are kept apart by this impartial method.

But unfortunately we cannot practice that principle in our workplace. Decisions that favor one person over another cannot be avoided. Giving accountable reasons helps to remove personal offense from those decisions. When we have listened carefully, our answers are more reasonable because we have looked through another set of eyes.

We need not fear making decisions. We need only fear making decisions before listening.

Lord, help me to become a patient listener.
Help me to see my world through Your eyes.

36
Truth

A false witness will not go unpunished, and he who pours out lies will not go free. . . . A false witness will not go unpunished, and he who pours out lies will perish. (vv. 5, 9)

Why are we tempted to lie? By the time we become young women we know that lying doesn't pay. Haven't we experienced a lie's coming back to haunt us? the stress of wondering if the fabrication will be found out? the worry that the real circumstances will surface?

Most of us shy away from outright lying, and we are somewhere between uncomfortable and downright miserable if we twist the truth. Yet we still experience a lingering temptation to make slight adjustments away from accuracy.

Jeremiah 17:9 tells us that the heart is deceitful, desperately wicked, and unpredictable. God created our hearts in His image, but when Eve and Adam chose to disregard God's instructions, human hearts became deceitful—like a magnet pulling facts until they are distorted.

I experience two great magnets of distortion: the desire for freedom and the desire to elevate myself.

Have you ever thought you could earn more money if you could lie? One young girl's father falsified her birth certificate in order for her to get a job serving drinks when she was sixteen. Child labor laws are violated, sometimes with parental consent, so that young people can earn a paycheck. We twist the truth in public education. We want our results to look better or desire funding for special programs, so we carefully select statistics to achieve our objective. In many areas, the facts are not always what we'd like them to be.

Many desirable goals, such as funding for a project or approval for a promotion, appear to be accessible if we would only lie. Money, power, position, prestige all become tangled as we twist the truth. Secretary of State James Baker, having been in high level government offices for nine years, stated that having a position of power does not bring inner security or fulfillment.

Wealth does not free us, as the dissatisfied, rich young ruler in Luke 18:18-24 illustrates. Proverbs tells us that the liar will not go free. Financial independence, which our society tells us is freedom, is not ultimate satisfaction. No ceiling on our credit card, no limits on our checking account will not produce a clear conscience before God and people, the ultimate freedom. "You will know the truth, and the truth will make you free" (John 8:32).

"The lamp of the Lord searches the spirit of a man; it searches out his inmost being" (Proverbs 20:27). When God searches us and finds truth, we experience ultimate freedom.

Have you ever thought people would like you better if they didn't know the real you? We revise our backgrounds, our family of origin, our philosophies. In fact, we'll agree with all kinds of opinions to get a nod of approval. Though we often think of false witnesses in relation to other people, we can be false witnesses of ourselves. When Proverbs speaks of the false witness perishing, perhaps the most painful death is when we haven't been truthful about ourselves, when we try to

99

live a lie. This seems to be a sin in good standing even among us as Christian working women. We try to pretend we're something we're not.

Why is it so difficult to let people know the real me? God made me and is so committed to my becoming all He intended that He gave up His only Son for me. Why should I not accept who I am and walk in God-pride before the world? Why do I need to bear false witness about myself?

I am a woman created by God. My heart is deceitful, but as God's daughter, with His help, I can be truthful. I can acknowledge my strengths and weaknesses. God sees the real me, and His is the opinion that matters.

Lord, create in me a clean heart
that is unresponsive to the magnet of twisting the truth.

37
Poverty

He who is kind to the poor lends to the Lord, and
he will reward him for what he has done. (v. 17)

Help often goes to those who can help themselves. I recently investigated new legislation along these lines. Bills were passed with help from strong lobbyists, vocal constituents, and people able to support their representatives. Most of these bills benefited a privileged population. That is the American way. Democratic, yes; the voice of the people, almost. Poor people were underrepresented in the list of new legislation.

Who are the poor? Jesus told us that we would always have poor people. How true. Even in our high-tech country, we have hungry and homeless people, people with inadequate health care, people for whom life, liberty, and especially the pursuit of happiness are not available.

The federal poverty level for a family of three is $13,380. Forty percent of all women who work full-time earn less than $15,000. One-third of female-headed families have poverty-level income. In other words they are the working poor. Every day in America 1,295 teenagers give birth. Most of these children are born into poverty. In our country twenty-seven children die every day from poverty.

We working women may have many demands on our paychecks. We may feel we cannot give large donations to help feed the world and house the homeless. But we can begin where we are with what we have; we need not look far to find those we can help. As we earn paychecks, let us hope we will look to the children, and their needy mothers, with compassion. We may be able to influence legislation and help voice the needs of the poor. We can help in other ways, too. We can encourage our churches to address the great need for quality care for little ones. We can teach our children that there is no harder or more important task than caring for another person. We must teach our children how important it is not to create another person until they are ready for that great responsibility.

We can promote fairness in the marketplace to narrow the twenty-nine cent difference on the dollar between men's and women's average earnings, a discrepancy especially difficult for female-headed households.

Will all these efforts make life, liberty, and the pursuit of happiness available to all? No. Jesus said we would always have the poor with us. But we might provide a keyhole of opportunity for a little person, we might let in a ray of hope for a sister who is sick and tired of being sick and tired. We might break the chain of generational poverty by providing training for one young girl before she begins parenting.

What if our efforts bring no apparent results, result in no return on our investment, no personal benefit, no community trophy? God Himself will reward us when we help the poor. Proverbs does not tell us how or when. Eternity is soon enough, and anything from His hand would be better than the best a nation or king could offer here on earth.

Lord, open my eyes to the poor around me.
Then open wide my heart, my hands,
and my wallet in compassion.

38
Seasons

A sluggard does not plow in season; so at harvest time he looks but finds nothing. (v. 3)

Seasons remind me with vivid color and mysterious power that God has created the world with order. As I write, plump buds on the trees outside my window are on the verge of bursting. The late March wind scuttles the last fall's few leaves over the hill, and the creek is escaping its boundaries again.

Nature has its seasons, with appointed times for rain, planting, harvesting, and resting. God asserts His sovereignty over all, but within His established order He has ordained variety and distinctiveness. Our lives are similar. We have seasons in which particular appointments are kept.

We sometimes forget this. Our world has become so chaotic that we sometimes disregard God's seasons and then wonder why we're in a fix. Some people do win the lottery instead of planting and harvesting. Infants die. The unpredictable does happen, but that does not negate God's order.

Solomon describes it clearly:

There is a time for everything
and a season for every activity under heaven:

a time to be born and a time to die,
a time to plant and a time to uproot,
a time to kill and a time to heal,
a time to tear down and a time to build,
a time to weep and a time to laugh,
a time to mourn and a time to dance,
a time to scatter stones and a time to gather them,
a time to embrace and a time to refrain,
a time to search and a time to give up,
a time to keep and a time to throw away,
a time to tear and a time to mend,
a time to be silent and a time to speak,
a time to love and a time to hate,
a time for war and a time for peace.

(Ecclesiastes 3:1-8)

You and I are in our planting season—work. We reap the harvest of a paycheck, barter coupons, or some kind of return. Are you tempted to consume the harvest in spring season? I am, and credit allows me to do so. Proverbs reminds me to plow in season if I want to harvest later. I am to till my field before building my house, to keep my level of living within my earning power. Many of the frustrations in life happen when we don't observe God's seasons.

Our affinity for speed encourages us to ignore areas of our lives related to seasons. We neglect mending relationships when tearing has occurred. We allow ourselves time to weep but not time to laugh; we cut mourning short because we must work. We forget to embrace; we try to build too quickly.

God did not create seasons for our frustration. They are good for body, soul, and spirit. Observing them preserves our health and welfare. Sometimes our sanity is also at stake. In the process of observing His seasons a miracle occurs. Our hurrying habits learn perseverance and patience. Growing up on the farm, I observed that you couldn't plant until the river bottom dried out. Tomato picking couldn't wait until after a hard frost. Maybe farmers find it easier to see God's sovereignty.

As a working woman I need to be reminded that God is the orderly controller of all events. I am thankful that He has given me seasons as evidence of His power in the universe. If He can transform this bleak hill to a shaded haven in His season, He can order my world.

Lord, help me conform to Your seasons in my life.

39
Old Age

The glory of young men is their strength, gray hair the splendor of the old. (v. 29)

Prime. The best cut, the highest rate, the best years. When we speak of best years we think young. Prime means energy, strength, ideas. In our culture, teens think you've lost it if you are over thirty. Some of us think they are right when we find ourselves peering into the refrigerator and can't remember why we opened the door.

God has a different view of prime. He speaks of old age as a stage to be desired. "Honor your father and mother—which is the first commandment with a promise—that it may go well with you and that you may enjoy long life on the earth" (Ephesians 6:2). Who wants "long life on the earth" if it means downhill after thirty?

Many good things come only with time. Wisdom is one of them. We can acquire knowledge quickly with focused effort. But wisdom comes through living with that knowledge, through the experience of fleshing out knowledge in our work, relationships, and survival.

Experience: the process of knowing, trying, experimenting, facing failure, tasting success—the stuff through which gray hairs are earned. This value comes with years, and only with years. Your prime is not necessarily your youth.

Strength and boundless energy are the crowns of youth, but not all that is important in life requires these. In this information age, many tasks require little muscle and much mind. If you are a woman reentering the marketplace or changing careers, this is encouraging news. You have experience, probably in many areas. There is a place for you.

What comes with age? Since we live in a sin-racked world and are sinful people, nothing is guaranteed. But if we live by godly principles (which is the whole point of Proverbs) some benefits in life will be natural results.

Wisdom must be first on the list. "Ears that hear and eyes that see—the Lord has made them both" (v. 12). Years of hearing and seeing bring perspective that no other person can give you.

"Mom, I will do it myself," we hear our children say. I have noticed that young parents with one child think they know a good deal about child-rearing. The more children a couple has and the older the children are, the quieter those parents become. However, these parents are precisely the ones to whom I gravitate with my questions. I learn from them because wisdom has opened their ears and eyes.

If you need information or advice on how to get something done in your job, go to the person who has worked on a similar project. The vintage secretary or custodian may help you. Prime thinking may be camouflaged behind graying hair and wrinkles.

We can seek out Christians who've lived with the Lord to talk through our plans. But wisdom is only ours when we've lived it ourselves.

Have you noticed that older people have time for the important? Grandpa has time to walk at a four-year-old pace around the neighborhood. Grandma has time to read the longest stories. Our elders seem to realize that the important will get done, and it needn't all happen yesterday. Perhaps that is an advantage of losing our strength and some of our energy. We slow down enough to get close to people.

Faithfulness is another characteristic acquired with age. It's easy to be a friend for a short time when the sun shines. "A man of many companions may come to ruin, but there is a friend who sticks closer than a brother" (18:24). One doesn't learn the truth of sticking closer than a sister without crisis, those hard times that must be endured or outlived, those moments where desertion is an option. This friendship principle applies in marriage and may apply also in the marketplace. Some co-workers are team people in the easy days but are hard to be found when the pressure increases or complications arise.

Years of living can teach us to be persistent. Rome wasn't built in a day, and neither are godly character, lasting relationships, or a successful career. The impulsiveness of youth gives way to persistence, a characteristic worth nurturing in our jobs, in our commitment to friends and relatives, and in our prayers.

We need not face the coming years with remorse or dread. A friend and I joked about wearing longer skirts for practicality, higher necklines and scarves to cover age spots, and lower heels for comfort. The reflection in the mirror is changing as we age. God sees it as splendor, the glory of nature as it reflects the goodness of God. I'd rather have that beauty than "prime"!

Lord, help me look at tomorrow and the coming years
as times of adventure
in which I can see Your goodness reflected in my life.

40
Sacrifice

All a man's ways seem right to him, but the Lord weighs the heart. To do what is right and just is more acceptable to the Lord than sacrifice. (vv. 2-3)

How can I please God? Do you ever wonder if you have anything to give to God? Much of our time and energy goes into our job. Many of us have families to whom we give less time and energy than we'd like. We give time to providing a roof over our head, bread on the table, and a little support for the body of believers. We feel spread thin.

But we hear that God wants our best, our all. How can I give to God, to work, and to loved ones? Is there enough of me to go around?

"With what shall I come before the Lord and bow down before the exalted God? Shall I come before him with burnt offerings, with calves a year old? Will the Lord be pleased with thousands of rams, with ten thousand rivers of oil? Shall I offer my firstborn for my transgression, the fruit of my body for the sin of my soul?" (Micah 6:6-7).

Sometimes I think that what I give to God is only valuable to Him if it hurts me, but this view of God is twisted. It inspires slashed bodies, infant sacrifice, extreme deprivation. Another view is that if God asks for a little, He'd really be happy with a lot. The Pharisees made great display of their giving. They tithed even the tiny grains of spices, not just their flocks of thousands.

We also combine these two views and believe God will only smile on us if we volunteer many hours of service for the body of believers. Or we believe He can only bless us if our financial gift to the poor is large. Or we think we need large amounts of devotional time with Him. If a vial of oil is a pleasing gift, then a river of oil will be a pleasing sacrifice, we say to ourselves. These views blend well with our culture that leans to excesses. Just as we thrive on conspicuous consumption and conspicuous spending, we think God likes conspicuous sacrifice.

"And what does the Lord require of you? To act justly and to love mercy and to walk humbly with your God" (Micah 6:8b). He wants me to walk with Him! My gifts are not as important as myself. What refreshing news for the Christian working woman! He wants me to be just—meaning right before God. I can be just as I work, parent, volunteer. Rather than a layer of sacrifice on top of everything else, God simply wants a God-directed heart.

He wants me to love mercy. One meaning of this word is "mutual liability of those belonging together." Freedom of decision is essential according to that definition. Mercy is an ethically binding relationship between relatives, hosts, allies, friends, or rulers. One who is in a position to help does so of her free will. It is the "how" in all my relationships, not a separate, additional thing that I do. Mercy is fidelity in my covenant relationships.

I am reassured that God is fully aware of all that I do and does not care to extract a punitive pound of flesh. Giving from my paycheck and helping when I can gives me pleasure. But His greatest satisfaction is to have me choose to walk beside Him. He delights in

my living in all my covenant relationships with justice
and mercy.

Lord, let's walk.

41
Responsibility

The horse is made ready for the day of battle, but victory rests with the Lord. (v. 31)

The saying "God helps those who help themselves" is bad news if you are helpless and weak. But if you are strong and competent it sounds great. Books have been written on God's responsibility versus man's responsibility, but I see it as too simplistic to claim all is one or the other. If all is man's responsibility, we deify ourselves and pretend we have characteristics we don't. Regardless of our strength, wealth, or influence some circumstances and forces are beyond our control.

If all were God's responsibility, we could become sluggards. Yet we know that is not His desire. Proverbs teaches that when we can do nothing He acts on our behalf. "Do not exploit the poor because they are poor and do not crush the needy in court, for the Lord will take up their case and will plunder those who plunder them" (22:22-23). Throughout Scripture we see God providing for widows, such as Ruth and Naomi, and watching over the adopted, such as Moses and Joseph.

My daily challenge is to live in the balance between God's omniscience as sole controller and power of the universe and my personal accountability. Proverbs 21:30 tells me, "There is no wisdom, no insight, no plan that can succeed against the Lord." Have you ever faced an insurmountable barrier at work? Perhaps an important project is thwarted, the budget is cut, or a supervisor says no. To be wise is to acknowledge that all outcomes are permitted by God: the job I have, the place I live, my means of transportation, the success of my projects, my stymied ideas.

When I am confused about what is my part and what is God's part, I ask myself this question: "Is my concern about this project or problem coming between God and me or drawing me closer to Him?" When Mary and Martha had dinner guests, Martha was distracted by the preparations (cf. Luke 10:40). When Jesus told the parable about a sower He talked about seed sown among thorns that did not produce a crop. He explained that that seed sown among thorns was the person who hears the Word but allows the worries of this life and the deceitfulness of wealth to choke it (cf. Matthew 13:22).

Much of life is a battle, and we sometimes find ourselves consumed by readying our horse. That is important but only as a means of winning the battle for the Lord. If we worry through the preparations and are distracted from living with kindness, patience, and thoughtfulness, glorifying God in the battle is unlikely.

God warned the children of Israel through Hosea that the battle would go against them "because you have depended on your own strength and on your many warriors" (Hosea 10:13b). I must pray, "Lord, will You give me the resources to accomplish this? Will You move the people I cannot move? What can I do to further Your kingdom in this situation? Using the gifts You have given me and the strength You provide, I think I have done what I can. I trust You to carry on—and I know You don't need my worrying to help You."

Lord, lift my eyes
from the distractions of this battle to You.

42
Mockers

Drive out the mocker, and out goes strife; quarrels and insults are ended. (v. 10)

Describe what your work environment would be like if there were no quarrels, strife, or insults. We would hardly call it work anymore if those clouds were absent. Proverbs tells us these problems are caused by mockers. Yet I had never thought of a mocker as such a bad person. I thought she was a nuisance, but not evil.

Looking through Proverbs, however, I learn that the mocker is not merely a nuisance to be ignored. The author uses the word in several places, presenting an alarming portrait: she scorns and mocks sin (14:9), is proud and haughty (21:24), is incorrigible (9:7), resists all reproof (9:8; 15:12), hates any rebuke (13:1), is odious to all men (24:9). Her chief characteristic is pride. "I have it; you don't."

No wonder she cannot be taught, does not take suggestions, looks down on others, and is obnoxious! Her opposite is the humble person. A humble person can be taught because she listens and therefore learns. She does not think of herself more highly than she ought. Paul tells us, "Think of yourself with sober judgment, in accordance with the measure of faith God has given you" (Romans 12:3). If we begin to push ourselves ahead of others and look down on them, the following verses can help us regain perspective.

"So, if you think you are standing firm, be careful that you don't fall!" (1 Corinthians 10:12) "Who are you to judge someone else's servant? To his own master he stands or falls. And he will stand, for the Lord is able to make him stand" (Romans 14:4). Why look for the speck in someone else's eye when your vision is impaired by a beam in your own? "So then, each of us will give an account of himself to God" (Romans 14:12).

When I too coolly evaluate someone else, thinking critically about who she is and what she does, I am in danger of becoming a mocker. If I am tempted to rank myself above others, whether at work, church, home, or in my community, I am in danger of becoming a mocker. On the heels of my critical evaluation is likely to come quarreling, strife, and insults.

What kind of woman do you respect at work? The woman who has it all? can do anything? looks perfect on a pedestal? Probably not. I admire a woman who knows her strengths and uses them, who acknowledges her weaknesses and is secure enough that she doesn't need to hide them. This woman allows the rest of us to be less than perfect but also allows us to excel without mocking us.

How can I be like this? Jesus was the perfect example. He was God Himself, but did not consider equality with God something to be grasped. He made Himself nothing and humbled Himself to the extent of dying on the cross. If I could follow a small portion of His example of humility, I would never become a mocker. "Do nothing out of selfish ambition or vain conceit but in humility consider others better than [more important than] yourselves. Each of you should look not only to your own interests, but also to the interests of others" (Philippians 2:3-4). Following Christ's example would rid our workplace of mockers.

Lord, replace my pride with humility.

43
Fear

The sluggard says, "There is a lion outside!" or,
"I will be murdered in the streets!" (v. 13)

The Reasonable Excuse

I didn't know it was due today.
The computer is slow this week.
I thought that was her job.
I think our base line data wasn't accurate.
We were so busy.
What do they expect, paying us so little?
I've not been feeling well.
Someone switched the in and out baskets.
I'm not trained for that.

Reasonable excuses are sometimes true. Your boss may not be able to distinguish truth from excuse. In Solomon's day, sometimes there were lions on the loose, and sometimes people were murdered in the streets. But not often. There was a grain of validity in the sluggard's fear. But not enough to justify his hibernating.

We can find excuses to cover our fears. Have you ever exaggerated the size of a project to justify waiting to begin? *I don't have time today to begin THAT!* Do you fear expending an all-out effort at work? *What if my best efforts fail? I'll tackle a safe, manageable project instead.* We can fear to flesh out a creative idea. We can fear to delegate authority. We can fear success.

Christian working women have a source of security to overcome our fears that other women don't have. We have the empowering Holy Spirit to help us utilize our God-given strengths and abilities (Romans 12:6-8). We have a promise that He will not bring temptation into our lives without providing a way for us to stand up under it (1 Corinthians 10:13). We are reassured that He will not condemn us when we try but fail (Romans 8:28-38). We are worthwhile whether we are multi-talented or have only one talent (1 Corinthians 12). Christian working women have a great resource in our God to be great risk-takers!

What happens when we put our hand to the plow? The principle I see in Scripture is this: when we use what is in our hand, He multiplies it. David used his slingshot and became competent with a giant-sized sword. The steward who invested ten talents was given cities to oversee. Moses' shepherd staff became the scepter of leadership. "Do you see a man skilled in his work? He will serve before kings; he will not serve before obscure men" (Proverbs 22:29).

When we do our work well, usually it is noticed. A well-carved chair becomes a treasured antique. A functional plan is implemented. Our ethical decisions are noted. Yet in our twisted world, this is not always the case. Christian working women have a King who always notices. He sees our effort, our faithfulness, our stepping out on risk's edge. We work before the King of Kings.

Lord, remove the lions
lurking in my mind and emotions.
I want to serve in God-pride before You,
unrestricted by fears.

44
Wealth

Do not wear yourself out to get rich; have the wisdom to show restraint. Cast but a glance at riches, and they are gone, for they will surely sprout wings and fly off to the sky like an eagle. (vv. 4-5)

Comparing riches to an eagle provides a contrast of opposites. Good and evil reside in both. The eagle combines swiftness, strength, and caring for its young with destructiveness as it preys on smaller animals. What an accurate mirror of wealth. Riches speed transactions. Money talks rapidly. Riches provide strength in the sense of power to provide goods, services, and influence. Riches can masquerade as a safety net, much like a nest for a family; they can be used to provide for others, to care for the needy, to further the work of the kingdom.

But wealth has a destructive side. We can love money rather than the good it can finance. We can transfer our trust from God to the things money buys: stocks, real estate, investments. Riches tempt giving hearts to become greedy. The vulture-like tendencies of wealth can overpower its virtues.

Proverbs reminds us that riches are quickly gone. David compared the speed of Saul and Jonathan to an eagle. This soaring bird can press its wings against its sides and power-dive, taking victims by surprise and bringing instant death. The golden eagle being chased by falcons was clocked at 120 miles an hour. Riches can change equally rapidly from assets to distraction that separate us from God.

We may not consider our paychecks riches, but small or large we see the dollars disappear like butter on a hot griddle. How we spend our dollars reveals what we value. Verse 6 reminds us that we can be stingy, while pretending to be generous. If we count the mouthfuls our guest consumes, the vulture side of wealth emerges. There is a difference between accountability and greed, between generosity and calculated investment.

The wise woman builds her house and fills its rooms with rare and beautiful treasures (24:3-4). Rather than being an admonition to splurge, this means precious and pleasant rooms. It speaks of rare means of intrinsic worth, quality, not quantity. Beautiful means lovely, agreeable, sweet. I have a treasure in my home. It is an antique chair that my sister acquired at an auction. My husband and I reupholstered it, carefully using the original 100-year-old-tacks. My son John once made a shelf that I consider more valuable than that chair, though it wouldn't produce much excitement at an auction. You may treasure a comfortable, well-used, expensive leather chair or a one-dollar footstool discovered at a flea market. What a wise woman accumulates reflects her values.

God's treasure is not determined by dollar value but by intrinsic worth. Consider what God describes as precious: wisdom (Proverbs 3:15), the steadfast love of God (Psalm 36:7), the death of His saints (Psalm 116:15), words of knowledge (Proverbs 20:15), the lives of oppressed people (Psalm 72:14), and you and me (Psalm 49:7). None of these can be contained in a room of plaster and wood, or codified and measured on an asset sheet. Yet all are riches that last. Having just one of those treasures—the steadfast love of God—is enough to make us wealthy women.

Lord, may I use my paycheck
to bring pleasantness to my surroundings
and invest in what is precious to You.

45
Family Matters

The father of a righteous man has great joy; he who has a wise son delights in him. May your father and mother be glad; may she who gave you birth rejoice! (vv. 24-25)

We were part of a rare celebration recently—the fiftieth anniversary of my husband's parents. In the midst of our hustling, mobile, superficial society, friends and relatives gathered, celebrated, and gave thanks for the miracle of family. Words cannot convey the faith that brought the two of them together—she who had experienced security and hard-working parents, he who had experienced his father's death at age eight and had felt the hunger of the depression. These two became one throughout ten moves, an aborted career, ministry, and beginning college when the family had become four.

Memories included relating an overheard comment from a doctor that Mother wouldn't make it through the night due to infection after a cesarean section. Yet she celebrated with her husband forty-eight years and two children later.

Perhaps the miracle of the day was not remembering their remarkable lives of faith but the impact on the eight assembled grandchildren as they heard what marriage really is. God's unique institution of family is indeed a miracle. Leaving and cleaving is only possible with Him.

As a working woman, I fear the loss of these celebrations and the demise of intergenerational relationships. Our days are full, and stresses in marriage are intensified by dual careers. Hours to celebrate family are crunched by our work.

Proverbs speaks of intergenerational pride, a diminishing quality in our individualistic culture. Something is accomplished in families that we can't accomplish on our own. We learn to accept one another's weaknesses, love covers our blunders, we lean on one another's strengths, we create a haven, a recovery room where family can be refreshed, energized for our work. Let's not lose this vision of family.

We are to listen to our fathers and not despise our mothers, an easier assignment for distant relatives than those nearest us. We can be critical; it's easy to dwell on family flaws. A vital strength can be a source of evil. Differences can evolve from how, when, and with whom we celebrate holidays, from finances and inheritance and dividing. And so it has been since sin entered the world in Genesis 3.

The end of this chapter of Proverbs addresses the sin of addiction. As I counsel adolescents I see the reality of the observation "In the end it bites like a snake and poisons like a viper" (v. 32). Some addictions are facilitated in families. Children hunger for security, which is hard to find when a parent is addicted. Children hunger for a safe, predictable environment—hard to find when the addiction is alcohol, overspending, gambling, or drugs. Whether an inherited tendency or environmentally encouraged, family makes a difference.

Family are the people who know us; family are the people who can intervene and confront. Families can provide the cause or the solution. If external forces trigger addiction, families can be sources of confrontation and natural consequences.

If you are part of a family, nurture and treasure those relationships. List the positives of which you can be proud. What looks ordinary to the world is extraordinary when commitment is respected, and honoring a covenant with tenacious commitment is not ordinary today.

Lord, help me to be a positive, committed person
for the generation that follows.

46
Stumbling

If you falter in times of trouble, how small is your strength! . . . For though a righteous man falls seven times, he rises again. (vv. 10, 16a)

I wish I were a spiritual giant, but in fact I am quite average. I am a saint by definition because I am a Christian, but I am considerably less than that in behavior. We have not received glorified bodies yet, and we have but a small portion of the mind of Christ.

I can falter and fall, but I rise again. As I investigated these words in the Hebrew, I found a difference between faltering and falling. The word *falter* means to sink down or be disheartened. It is the term used in Isaiah 5:24, "as dry grass sinks down in the flames." It is letting go, giving in, succumbing to circumstances.

Do you ever feel like letting go and just sinking down and giving in to the circumstances? I felt like that yesterday when the transmission went out on my van. The day before, our ten-year-old beast-car had died. I wanted to write, not call tow trucks, compare repair bills, and discover one was worth $25 and the other needed $800 to coax it to run again. Meanwhile how would I get to work?

On a more serious note, I have felt like giving up as a Christian woman. When I see my failures as a parent, my impatience in my work, my personal less-than-godly desires, I want to sink down. Faltering is an internal problem.

Falling is different. This refers to external circumstances that trip us up. We may become weary or get down, but our legs are still pumping. We're on the way up because we haven't given up. The falterer is in trouble but the righteous woman who has fallen will rise again. There is a difference.

Both experience adversity. Living in this world means times of trouble and anguish. David wept over the death of Jonathan. Job suffered every possible loss a man could experience. Shadrach, Meshach, and Abednego could have faltered in the furnace. But God's three witnesses did not sink in the flames; they trusted God to deliver them. Working women face adversity in their jobs, career crises, personal injury, and financial bankruptcy.

Whether I falter and give up or fall and rise again does not depend on the difficulty of my circumstances or the intensity of the temptation. It depends on what I believe about God. I believe His power raised Jesus from death to life. I believe I will live again in a life after this with the creator of the universe. I believe Jesus is pleading my case with God in the insignificant nuisances as well as the adversities that test me to the core.

"For I am convinced that neither death nor life, neither angels nor demons, neither the present nor the future, nor any powers, neither height nor depth, nor anything else in all creation, will be able to separate us from the love of God that is in Christ Jesus our Lord" (Romans 8:38-39).

Amen, Lord.

47
National Accountability

Whoever says to the guilty, "You are innocent"—
peoples will curse him and nations denounce
him. (v. 24).

In our individualistic society, we sometimes forget
that we are part of a bigger picture, that we are a nation. In Solomon's day, government and religion were
one and the same. God's rules were the religious leaders' rules and the nation's rules. The scene has obviously changed dramatically. Though our laws supposedly do not interfere with our religious freedom, policies
sometimes challenge our faith; laws occasionally dis-
courage biblical living.

Still, there is a sense of right and wrong in much
of our world. Nations are still incensed by meaningless
killing and torture. World groups assemble to discour-
age savage behavior and protect helpless people, at
least to some extent.

Though God deals with us as individuals, He also
recognizes us corporately, as a nation. To the extent
that our group standards follow His policies, we will be
blessed as a group. The Old Testament documents two
thousand years of this.

The advice that appears at the end of this chapter
of Proverbs illustrates this point. The text could be
paraphrased, "Finish your outdoor work and get your
fields ready; after that, build your house." Establish

your work, see your product or profit, and then determine how you will live, or your standard of spending. This guideline for personal living is applicable as a national policy as well. Personal debt may indicate personal greed; national debt may indicate national greed. Our greed may deprive our children of life, liberty, and the pursuit of happiness as we know it today. Our care of the earth will affect the future if we do not consider pollution and its long-range effects.

"Do not testify against your neighbor" (v. 28). We prosper if we get along with each other. We will hopefully see more prosperity in Europe with the destruction of the Berlin wall. Shared resources, shared knowledge, and communication benefits all. Nations benefit, as do neighborhoods, when we communicate.

"I went past the field of the sluggard." What a picturesque description of unused, neglected resources. Facing hunger and poverty, some groups seem powerless to provide for themselves. We can do as Solomon did and let our hearts be touched by what we observe. God has created a world that can abundantly feed all if we live by His principles. We can share knowledge, demonstrate skills, and exercise compassion because poverty and scarcity have lurked ever since sin entered the world.

I feel small as I consider nations of hungry people and women who cannot read, cannot control reproduction, cannot feed their children. I can only order my world to a small extent. I cannot expect my country to live by principles I only give lip service to but do not live by. "Seek the Lord, all you humble of the land, you who do what he commands" (Zephaniah 2:3). I can begin in my small sphere of influence. I can vote, pray, and flesh out godly principles.

Lord, guide us
through personal righteousness and corporate right living
to become a nation that honors You.

48
Pride

These are more proverbs of Solomon, copied by the men of Hezekiah king of Judah. . . . As the heavens are high and the earth is deep, so the hearts of kings are unsearchable. (vv. 1, 3)

Ten kings reigned over Judah between Hezekiah and Solomon. Solomon's wisdom was probably passed from one generation to another. Hezekiah decided that it should be recorded, and he commissioned scribes for the task. This is not surprising. "Hezekiah trusted in the Lord, the God of Israel. There was no one like him among all the kings of Judah, either before him or after him. He held fast to the Lord and did not cease to follow him; he kept the commands the Lord had given Moses" (2 Kings 18:5-6).

Hezekiah exercised bold faith in declaring war, calling on God's power for victory, and returning his people to the worship of God. "So that all kingdoms on earth may know that you alone, O Lord, are God" (2 Kings 19:19). When Hezekiah was near death, his prayer for healing touched God's heart. God secured His promise to give him fifteen more years of life by moving the shadow backwards. Hezekiah's early reign was characterized by bold faith, direct prayer, and motivation to glorify God.

But something changed with Hezekiah's healing. Such an act of God can inspire praise and humility or pride and haughtiness. Sadly, Hezekiah chose the latter. "Admirers" from Babylon heard of his illness and came bearing gifts. Hezekiah showed them his nation's entire storehouse—weapons of war and wealth. A leader might do that for an ally, but that was hardly the relationship between Babylon and Judah. No doubt Hezekiah strode with pride through those treasures, able to walk due to God's healing but walking proud before his fall.

The prophet Isaiah confronted him and gave him God's judgment: the Babylonians would carry off all they had seen, and Judah would become their captives. Had the king heard this judgment before his healing, perhaps he would have wept and pleaded for his people. As a humble king, he had gone to war to protect his subjects and he had cleaned up the twisted mess of so-called worship he had inherited. He wanted the earth to know that God alone was God.

But in his healed body his heart twisted, and he became concerned only about himself. He asked, "Will there not be peace and security in my lifetime?" (2 Kings 20:19) What disregard for family; his children would become slaves. What discredit to his God; his nation would crumble.

And yet he was the king who had recorded Solomon's words. "The hearts of kings are unsearchable." David wisely pleaded with God, "Turn my heart toward your statutes and not toward selfish gain. Turn my eyes away from worthless things; renew my life according to your word" (Psalm 119:36).

Sometimes when God has worked miraculously on our behalf we are tempted to become proud. Working women are not immune. Success can breed pride. Our nose tips up, our neck is unbending, and we feel pedestal-perfect. Inevitably our focus becomes self-centered. Learning from Hezekiah changes my prayer from, "Lord, heal at all costs" to, "Lord, heal if I can humbly walk with Your blessing." The truth applies to any request we make for God to work in our life. Boasting and blessing don't match.

Lord, Thy will be done.

49
Self-control

If you find honey, eat just enough—too much of it, and you will vomit. . . . Like a city whose walls are broken down is a man who lacks self-control." (vv. 16, 28)

We live in a time of extremes. Big is good, bigger is better, and biggest is great. Which tower is tallest in Chicago? Which Sunday brunch serves the greatest variety and most exotic table of delicacies?

Proverbs reminds us that a little of a good thing is often enough—a lesson hard to learn in our times. The difference between a healthy appetite and greed can be fatal. We want to drain every ounce of life, and sometimes we drink the dregs in doing so. God says, "Enough." We say, "More." Instead of ecstasy, we end up with nausea.

I remember going to the apple orchard as a child to buy bushels for canning. I dreaded the work to come, but one treat accompanied the hot, long job. We would buy a wide-mouthed mason jar filled with a chunk of honeycomb. In the midst of the work, Mama would make a skillet of biscuits. Nothing tasted better than that little dark stream dribbling from a chunk of comb on my biscuit. I never considered drinking the whole jar. But that's the American way. "Enough" at present may mean "too much" in the future. We may take on one more project at work because it is interesting or sounds stimulating. Weeks later when we are overwhelmed with the burden of that project in addition to our other tasks, we gasp, "Too much!"

We share the "enough is too much" principle jokingly with another couple who also have four children. When we each had two little ones, we enjoyed them so much, we each had two more. Enough, we thought. Recently we vacationed together with all eight teenagers. Our conclusion: we were living proof of the Peter Principle, which states that we rise one step above our abilities, therefore living and working at a level of incompetency. Sitting on the cabin deck with our coffee and sharing our challenges, failures, and dreams, we felt "enough is too much." We would not, of course, relinquish any of our children; we are committed to our covenant of parenting. But parenting occasionally illustrates that we commit ourselves beyond our comfort zone. Like that one extra dessert from the buffet, one more becomes too much.

We can get in over our heads. It is hard to foresee the future results of some of our decisions. If you're an impulsive, leap-before-you-look person, as I am, you know that enough can be too much.

Proverbs tells us that too much of a good thing is like a city whose walls are broken down. Walls are for protection. Limits are from the Lord. "A prudent wife is from the Lord" (19:14). Solomon himself had too many wives. They brought with them their strange religions, and his kingdom got out of control. Work is good. But when we take on too many projects, the physical and emotional consequences of that "enough" become too much for us.

"Lips that speak knowledge are a rare jewel" (20:15). Talk is cheap because supply exceeds demand. We must add one last comment—a comment that should have remained unsaid. "Seldom set foot in your neighbor's house—too much of you, and he will hate

132

you" (25:17). Benjamin Franklin put it more bluntly. "Fish and relatives stink after three days." Knowing when to stop builds a wall of protection around us. Self-control protects us from extremes.

I remember Grandpa McCoy bowing his head over a meager meal of boiled potatoes and turnips. His prayer of thanksgiving sounded as though he were seated before a feast of delicacies. If we were grateful for what we have, would our appetites be satiated? I think so. Thankfulness fills heart and soul, and enough feels like enough. "Better a little with the fear of the Lord than great wealth with turmoil" (15:16). Self-control is not easily acquired. But thankfulness for what God has provided is a good beginning.

Lord, thank You for rich dribbles of honey.

50
Initiative

The sluggard says, "There is a lion in the road."
. . . The sluggard buries his hand in the dish; he
is too lazy to bring it back to his mouth. The slug-
gard is wiser in his own eyes than seven men
who answer discreetly. (vv. 13a, 15-16)

Few working women are classic case sluggards. We don't have time for the "luxury" of laziness. But I see some of myself in the sluggard. She is anchored to her bed, and she has prolific excuses. It is hard to roll out on cold dark mornings, and I can think of several reasons to avoid doing disagreeable tasks.

The sluggard is characterized by some choice traits:

1. She will not begin things (v. 14)
2. She will not finish things (v. 15)
3. She will not face things (v. 13)

Do you find that the first step in a task is the hardest? One report that I must complete on students is especially tedious. I can postpone, postpone, and postpone case studies. Once I'm reading my Bible, I have no problem becoming engrossed in God's blessings. But sometimes reaching for my Bible is difficult. Stripping the first piece of wallpaper is easy to put off, but once the plaster dust is flying, redecorating is fun. Perhaps you dread monthly reports, taking inventory, or preparing your tax report. Often our greatest effort is required to take the first step.

Some of us are good beginners but not finishers. The effort of beginning is so great that we stop in midstream or become bored. Maybe you are an idea person. You can always devise a plan or a new method, but then you'd rather turn it over to someone else. It's easy if we have others to whom we can delegate responsibility, yet usually we're responsible for finishing what we start.

God sometimes assigns someone to be a beginner only, or a finisher only. We have examples in Scripture of beginners and finishers. David assembled supplies for the Temple. But God gave the job of building it to Solomon. Paul could say he'd fought the good fight, finished the race, because he was satisfied with his ministry. He did not begin as one of the original twelve apostles, but he completed his part of spreading the gospel. Regardless of which area is our strength, it is important that we not imitate the sluggard and do nothing.

The sluggard does not face things. She comes to believe her own excuses. Sometimes we are unsure of our decision-making abilities, especially if we're new in the marketplace, in a new job, or changing careers. So we avoid voicing an opinion, making a decision, or stating what we think. We rationalize to justify our silence or our nonactivity. But we should instead draw confidence from God's promise: "'For I know the plans I have for you,' says the Lord, 'plans to prosper you and not to harm you, plans to give you hope and a future'" (Jeremiah 29:11).

Do you ever feel that you can only face challenges from a position of strength, that you must feel secure and confident in your work? I sometimes face decisions with a sense of insecurity. If you also find yourself in this position, this is a passage to lean on: "Therefore, strengthen your feeble arms and weak knees. 'Make level paths for your feet,' so that the lame may not be disabled, but rather healed" (Hebrews 12:12-13).

God believes we can mark out a straight, firm path, even with shaky legs and quaking knees. Other women, including our co-workers, daughters, and friends, are following us and need our example. Remember the ant? She needs no overseer and is not hindered by obstacles. Remember the harvest? There are appointed times for starting and finishing. Take a new grip. There are others following us.

Lord, remove the sluggard in me.

51
Meddling

Like one who seizes a dog by the ears is a passer-by who meddles in a quarrel not his own. (v. 17)

Have you ever tried to help a co-worker only to find your input was unwelcome? Has your support or advice ever been misconstrued as meddling? Webster defines meddling as "interfering without right or propriety." Proverbs's advice on friendships can help us avoid interfering.

Three kinds of friendships are illustrated in Proverbs. The bosom companion sticks closer than a brother (18:24). This friend supports another's goals. In the Old Testament this friendship occasionally included betrayal, a lesson to show us that even the closest friendships need guarding. Relationships may appear unflappable, but they are not always what they seem. Bosom companions, like family, can confront. David shirked his duty to his son Adonijah, did not confront him, and his son died. Eli did not confront his sons on their sin, and they suffered. Relatives and close friends can help us avoid sin.

Casual friendships are abundant. They do not have the candor of close friendships, but they provide some counsel, encouragement, and pleasure. Whereas a close friend may confront ("faithful are the wounds of

137

a friend," 27:6, NASB*) casual friends go with the flow. The comfort of casual friendships is not necessarily ideal because they do not confront sin.

Acquaintances are those who cross our paths but don't walk in them. They are in our life but not of it. They are just passing by. When they become enmeshed in our issues it is meddling. A close friend or even a casual co-worker might legitimately be involved in our concerns. But an acquaintance's interference is the case of another cook stirring the stew.

If you want to get our black Labrador's attention, grab his ears. His reaction is quick, unpredictable, and never friendly. You have touched a sensitive area. We usually do not quarrel over those issues that do not matter to us. Casual friends or acquaintances becoming involved in something over which we are arguing guarantees touching sensitive areas. This territory is best trod only by close friends.

Sometimes office politics tempt us to meddle. We are drawn to become enmeshed in issues that are not our own. We may develop close friends at work, but frequent contact does not ensure friendship. We may mistakenly believe our input is welcome when it is not. Our wisest step may be to *ask* our co-worker or friend whether she would like our input on an issue. Honor her answer!

Grabbing our dog's ears accomplishes nothing. He cannot be directed or subdued, only irritated. Unless you are a person's friend, getting involved in her quarrel will accomplish nothing but irritation or agitation. Verse 21 describes the result: a fire is fed.

When we don't know someone well, our input can be inappropriate at best, hurting or destructive at worst. "Like one who takes away a garment on a cold day, or like vinegar poured on soda, is one who sings songs to a heavy heart" (25:20). An acquaintance says,

*New American Standard Bible.

"Cheer up," when your heart is breaking, or, "Everything will turn out fine," when you know the crisis will change your life, and you don't know if you can face that unknown.

In our workplace we learn discretion as to who are acquaintances and who are friends. Working desk-to-desk or office-to-office does not guarantee friendship. We cannot assume intimacy based on physical proximity. When we want to become involved in another's quarrel or decision we might ask ourselves, Will the issue be resolved or improved if I jump in? What is my motivation? Am I looking for more information? For what reason? Am I seeking to increase the intensity or excitement in my boring life? Our motivation may be less than pure.

The Pharisees asked Jesus questions to corner Him. Some people followed Him for free food. Judas stayed with Him for personal benefit. What is our motivation?

Lord, keep me busy doing good
so that I have no time for meddling.
Keep me pure so that I have no desire to do so.

52
Planning

Do not boast about tomorrow, for you do not know what a day may bring forth. (v. 1)

Sometimes we misread this verse to say, "Do not plan for tomorrow, for you do not know what a day may bring forth." Sometimes I wish it said that. Working women expend much mental energy planning. We do not have much flexible time; we have our work, we have living space to keep up, sometimes a vehicle to keep running. We have children, mates, friends, aging relatives. My wallet calendar is covered with yellow sticky lists: "grocery," "to do tonight," "must happen this weekend." I even have a "spare time" list. It includes optional activities such as window washing and sorting spring clothes. (Optional means it may happen every other year.)

We need not feel we are usurping God's authority by planning. He advises us to prepare our horse for battle. We are to "know the condition of [our] flocks" so we will "have plenty of goats' milk to feed [our families]" (vv. 23, 27). He knows our needs (Luke 12:28) and expects us to be accountable in providing for our own (1 Timothy 5:8).

Proverbs tells us the wise woman does not *boast* of her plans. Boasting displaces the God-factor with the I-factor. "See what I can accomplish; see the potential results of my strategic intelligence; see my fore-thought." Though plans are laudable, they can only be accomplished with God's hand of blessing, permission, or tolerance.

I can tell whether I'm depending on the God-factor or I-factor by my reaction to change and disruption. Have you ever noticed how many changes in your plans are due to factors beyond your control? You do not set all deadlines at work. You cannot prevent computer breakdowns. You are not directly responsible for irritable customers or clients who need extra time and explanation. Illness, accidents—much is beyond our control. I must lay my plans before the Lord and say, "These are subject to You. Change, bless, remove. Keep me from taking a step that will not honor You."

> Now listen, you who say, "Today or tomorrow we will go to this or that city, spend a year there, carry on business and make money." Why, you do not even know what will happen tomorrow. What is your life? You are a mist that appears for a little while and then vanishes. Instead, you ought to say, "If it is the Lord's will, we will live and do this or that." As it is, you boast and brag. All such boasting is evil. Anyone, then, who knows the good he ought to do and doesn't do it, sins. (James 4:13-16)

When I am frustrated by plans going askew, usually I need to slow down and ask myself, Why are you in such a dither, Miriam? By looking closely at what I really feel, I realize that I'm worried about not looking good if the plan doesn't go my way. Sometimes I fear losing control of the situation. I need to remind myself that events beyond my grasp are only to be feared if I don't believe God is big enough or caring enough to be in charge.

141

He tells me not to set my heart on what I will eat and drink, not to worry. "But seek his kingdom, and these things will be given to you as well" (Luke 12:31).

Lord, replace the I-factor with You.

53
Friendship

As iron sharpens iron, so one man sharpens another. (v. 17)

We watched a blacksmith at a colonial fair shape a horseshoe. A black rod glowed red-orange. With blows and twisting, gradually the rod took on a new form—a useful form for a new purpose. Then he transformed pieces into nails; bluntness became pointed—sharp and useful.

Proverbs tells us communication can be like that. We can sharpen each other. We can speak with candor, help each other think critically, see the world through different eyes.

Traditionally women have been good communicators. Tests show that our verbal skills develop early. We practice them, don't we? But sometimes I think that though we talk, we are not candid. We have difficulty expressing displeasure. We have difficulty communicating negative thoughts and feelings. Anger is especially hard to express because it may mask other feelings we'd rather not admit. Women also have difficulty receiving praise.

Proverbs tell us that "faithful are the wounds of a friend" (27:6, KJV*). Sometimes we'd rather be well-

*King James Version.

143

liked than faithful. We would rather keep the friendship superficial than risk wounding by honest communication. The ability to give and take correction is a badge of honor, a way we sharpen each other.

Anger is frequently a second-hand emotion. Often when we examine our anger, we find another emotion underneath that we'd rather not own. In denying the original emotion, we let anger masquerade for our true feelings. Often behind my anger is hurt. A friend hurts me, but I don't want her to know she is important enough to hurt me deeply. We are uncomfortable admitting intense feelings, so we get mad. It is easier to be angry than to be hurt. Yet if iron is to sharpen iron, we need to be candid and talk about what we feel. Scripture tells us to communicate the truth *in love*. This removes the combat and negative confrontation from being open. Honesty brings a new shape to the relationship.

Women who are able to sharpen each other accept their differences. I may start a support group for underachievers while another counselor works individually with those students. We can accept our differences and profit by sharing our methods.

Forgiveness needs to accompany our willingness to be open; forgiveness of others who are not always what we hoped they would be and forgiveness of ourselves when we react before considering the consequences. The greater our acceptance of our co-workers' differences, the less need for forgiveness.

Praise is equally difficult to communicate—to give and receive. We may think that by putting ourselves down we make others feel better. We may not esteem ourselves as God does and therefore cannot accept praise. "A man is praised according to his wisdom" (12:8). To be praised for wisdom is a compliment to God, the giver of wisdom. All that we have is from Him, so we accept praise on His behalf. Have you been praised for being creative? generous? thoughtful? diligent? a thorough thinker? Accept the praise on behalf of God who created you.

"Let another praise you, and not your own mouth" (27:2). Praise from a friend can sharpen us, reassure us, and build our God-confidence that He is using us. Praise changes our perspective. Knowing this, let us praise others more. "You're doing a good job." "I appreciated what you shared in the meeting." "I noticed that you went the extra mile on that project. Thanks."

We can expect iron sharpening iron to be painful sometimes. But moving beyond the superficial is part of becoming God's new creation.

Lord, help me
to communicate with others
as You communicate with me.

54
Leadership

Evil men do not understand justice, but those who seek the Lord understand it fully. (v. 5)

Are you a leader? Have you been promoted? Do others report to you? Proverbs illustrates the characteristics of justice. Leaders would do well to study them carefully and implement them where possible. An organization requires justice to be successful. Whether the organization is a company, nation, or family its members will thrive on the stability that justice provides.

Justice is impartial, providing a norm, a measuring rule, to which all can relate. Proverbs refers to honest weights and measures and to moral standards. In a just organization, those norms are practiced without partiality. They are applied equally to the rich and poor; they provide a basis of fairness for conduct between people. Expectations are clear, providing stability to the work environment.

Justice is reasonable; what is happening to others is important. If a company looks only at the bottom line dollar to measure success, policies can be unreasonable and people suffer. Justice reflects God's character and His concern for His people.

Sometimes we believe that if every aspect of goods and services that related to the interaction of people were spelled out in a clear law or policy, all problems would be solved. It's a nice thought, but it's not enough and clearly impossible. First, in any organization on earth some rules and regulations will contradict each other and some people will not be treated fairly. But let's assume that we could create fair laws. Would justice prevail? Even if every business transaction had a clear policy for implementation, people would be the facilitators, catalysts, and overseers—and people are sometimes unjust.

"Blessed is the man who always fears the Lord, but he who hardens his heart falls into trouble" (28:14). If the policies on the books were all perfect, we would still have the problem of human hearts. The hardened heart enforces a yoke that is hard to bear. The hardened heart refuses advice, counsel, and leading. And the best of rulers and leaders can harden their hearts.

Proverbs graphically tells us what happens with a hard-hearted leader: she destroys productivity (28:3), her prayers are not heard (v. 9), people go into hiding (v. 28), she tears down her organization (29:4), and people cast off restraint (v. 18).

Leaders' hearts are revealed when the people are helpless. The just leader with a compassionate heart gives to the needy, protects the poor, looks out for those who cannot help themselves. The hard-hearted leader oppresses the poor like a roaring lion or a charging bear (v. 15)

The condition of the organization, the state of the nation, and the needs of the kind of family do not determine the characteristics of the leader. Her characteristics are determined by her commitment to God. Though a leader may have the power to change the rules, depending on who stands before her, and though she may impose a hard yoke, she acts reasonably with impartiality and fairness because she serves a just God.

147

When we have the opportunity to lead and determine which standards we will follow we need to remember that there is no original authority on earth. All authority is designated, is secondhand. The Roman centurion recognized this. "For I myself am a man under authority" (Luke 7:8). He recognized that Jesus was exercising God's authority, a concept that even the Jews could not accept.

We can best exercise authority if we place ourselves under God. Only He can direct fair and just decisions. "Many seek an audience with a ruler, but it is from the Lord that man gets justice" (29:26).

Lord, shape my heart to lead as You do.

55
Honoring Parents

He who robs his father or mother and says, "It's not wrong"—he is partner to him who destroys. (v. 24)

God gave Moses ten basic rules for the foundation of Israel's new nation. Commandment number five was, "Honor your father and your mother, so that you may live long in the land the Lord your God is giving you" (Exodus 20:12). In spite of the volumes of law in our nation, we have none specifically related to our relationship or commitment to our parents. That absence speaks loudly.

The most frequent word Scripture uses to describe our parental relationship is *honor.* The word means weighty in the sense of being noteworthy or impressive. To give honor is to say they deserve respect, attention, and obedience. As children, we were to obey them because they were responsible for our care, teaching, and behavior. After becoming accountable adults, though we are responsible for our behavior, Scripture still directs us to treat our parents with respect. The issue of care reverses, and we become responsible for them. God considered this high priority. Consider Mark 7:9-13:

> And he said to them; "You have a fine way of setting aside the commands of God in order to observe

149

your own traditions! For Moses said, 'Honor your father and mother,' and, 'Anyone who curses his father or mother must be put to death.' But you say that if a man says to his father or mother: 'Whatever help you might otherwise have received from me is Corban' (that is, a gift devoted to God), then you no longer let him do anything for his father or mother. Thus you nullify the work of God by your tradition that you have handed down. And you do many things like that.

God considers care of parents more important than giving to Him. Jesus followed that speech with a harsh denunciation of hypocrisy. Isaiah denounced the children of Israel because they honored God with their lips but not with their actions. In my busy world, when I invest time and energy in my extended family, I am honoring God. Sharing my home with relatives may mean opening cans instead of baking time-honored traditional dishes, but time for togetherness is still important.

Often in Scripture an individual is honored for accomplishing a heroic feat. I am learning each day that parenting four teenagers is a heroic feat! Our country does not seem to value children and the policies of our companies are not often in children's best interests. We get precious little support and encouragement for parenting in our society. But God says parenting is an honorable feat! We acknowledge the high priority God places on parenting by honoring our parents.

Caring for another person is the most important job in the world. Perhaps you have said to your adolescent children, "Before you create a baby, make sure you are ready for such a special job." They can tell whether we mean what we say when they see us caring for our parents. Better to be known as the sandwich generation than the generation who neglected our parents.

150

I remember Mama giving Grandpa McCoy sponge baths before he died. His body showed many signs of death's approach, so it was not a pleasant job. We were too poor to pay for hospital care or extra help. A robin built its nest outside the bedroom window where he lay. In my child's mind, I thought God sent the robin so Grandpa would have beauty to watch that summer. When he died on Thanksgiving, I glimpsed my mother looking at that nest in the stark winter branches. A look of peace eased the fatigued stress in her face. Maybe God sent the robin to comfort her, to remind her that she had honored her father.

To rob our father and mother is to destroy them. To give honor to them is to gain something that can never be taken away.

Lord, thank You for Your fifth commandment.

56
Anger

A fool gives full vent to his anger, but a wise man keeps himself under control. (v. 11)

Do you ever wonder why God created you with the emotion of anger? It gets us into lots of trouble sometimes, doesn't it? Consider what's good about anger. It is one of the most energizing emotions. Adrenalin flows and we have great strength. Anger focuses our attention. Have you ever tried to read the newspaper while you were angry? To sleep? Teach a lesson? Concentrate on a project? Converse on an unrelated topic? Focused attention and energy—sounds like a good thing —unless your attention belongs elsewhere.

You and I know our anger does not always result in good. Anger can be our worst enemy. If we spew it, we hurt others or make a bad situation worse. If we shove it inside, we hurt ourselves.

"'In your anger do not sin': Do not let the sun go down while you are still angry, and do not give the devil a foothold" (Ephesians 4:26-27). This verse is reassuring. We can be angry and not sin. Jesus was. He was angry for the right reasons. He was angry when God was not honored. In His anger He drove the money changers out of the Temple because they were disrespecting God by misusing His special territory. If Christians consistently suppress anger they will no longer feel anger when it is appropriate, such as when God is not honored.

Ephesians shows us that anger should be a short-lived emotion. God, who created our bodies as well as our emotions, tells us to get rid of our anger before nightfall. Otherwise we can't sleep. Christian working women especially need this instruction. Our lives are full, and rest is important. If we have difficulty resolving anger before nightfall, fatigue intensifies our problem. How can we keep anger short-lived?

First we can look at our anger, admit our feelings, and decide whether we are angry for a justifiable reason. Is our anger a second-hand emotion? If we feel angry because we are hurt, we need to back up and deal with the hurt. We may need to forgive a fellow worker, friend, or relative. If anger is a first-hand emotion, why are we feeling it? What can we do about the cause? We can make a plan of what we need to do. Perhaps we should speak out for God's principles in our town, state, or workplace. The problem may remain unsolved. The money changers Jesus threw out may have continued dishonoring God in a new place. But Jesus had done God's will. The results were in God's hands.

Are you ever caught in a crunch where you feel God's principles are ignored in your workplace? We may have to conform to a less than ideal policy if we are powerless to change the policy or circumstance. However, if adhering to the policy would violate God's Word, we should remember Daniel. Ultimately, we want to please God.

Many times my anger is the result of my expecting something of people that they cannot deliver. If I expect them to give me esteem or to meet my needs beyond their willingness or capability, I will probably become angry. Humans have clay feet. Often I need to go to God and ask Him to meet those needs in a new way and to leave my expectations with Him, not others.

153

The workplace brings together clay-footed people. Projects are delayed, overtime may be required with or without pay, convenient or inconvenient. Rather than become angry, try repeating this mundane statement: Work is called work because it *is* work.

Proverbs tells us to keep ourselves under control. Self-control is an exercise that improves with practice: to wait before speaking, to ask myself, *Why?* to make a plan of how to direct my energy before nightfall, to lay my expectations at God's feet. These exercises will probably result in a good night's sleep.

Lord, thank You for my emotions.
Help me to exercise control and
direct them for positive living.

57
Maturity

Discipline your son, and he will give you peace;
he will bring delight to your soul. (v. 17)

If this were a devotional for parents, we could talk about the virtues of disciplining children. Do any of those truths have relevance to working women? There is a child in each of us. When we were small our parents taught that child. Now, as adults, we parent that child. Our inner child can be part of our strength or our weakness. How we parent her is strongly affected by the parenting we received as a child.

If we had few restraints, self-control may come with difficulty. If we had little affection, we crave acceptance. If we were not held accountable, we tend to be irresponsible. Three characteristics are especially strong in children: children are possessive, they are impulsive, and they believe the center of the universe is themselves. All of us—working women and working men—still have a child within us. We bring that child not only to our relationships, friends, mates, and children, but to the marketplace as well.

The possessive child in us says, "Mine!" We hoard our computer, our paper clips, our space, our ideas. The good side of this trait is taking ownership for our tasks and responsibility for our space, achieving a balance so that possessiveness does not interfere with our work. The possessive child in some adults hoards information. This desire for control results in secret-keeping that frustrates others or halts productivity. It is difficult to make a good presentation when you can't assemble all the data. Balanced decisions are impossible when you cannot access the facts.

Children act on impulse. At age six, I ate a woolly worm. It looked pretty and soft. I now know that those hairs sting and are for the worm's protection, not my taste buds. Sometimes our quick impulse results in pain for ourselves and others. We jump to erroneous conclusions. Discipline means teaching. We teach the inner child by giving her more information. The time invested in research, in learning about a person or project, is usually time well spent. The impulsive little girl inside us can be controlled by the experience of eating woolly worms or the discipline of learning. I prefer the latter.

We may also know those who research or analyze forever until opportunity is gone. Our inner child may be fearful of decision-making, fearful of being accountable for her decisions.

We jokingly call some children "princess." That may be a nice term for a young girl dressed in her finery. But have you ever had to work with one? I ask myself, Is there a little princess in me? If the project doesn't go her way, she sulks. Work proceeds on her timetable. Her tongue is quick to berate those who let her down. She clamors for attention and seldom encourages a spirit of cooperation.

Discipline means training, teaching. With children that takes time, commitment, and a recognition of the lessons that need to be learned. Consider creating some solitude; take some time and get to know the child in you. What training can you bring to her? How might you parent her? Accept her strengths and forgive her weaknesses, taking them to the Lord for change and blessing.

Proverbs tells us that a child can bring delight to your soul. What is delightful about your inner child? Most children are curious and want to participate. We took our boys to a football game where our daughter attends college. As we watched a field goal set up, I noticed the bleacher seat of my youngest was empty. The cheer went up for the successful kick. None other than Rob darted into the end zone and caught the football. He didn't want to warm the bleachers; he wanted to be in the game. Hopefully, the maturity that comes with age will not sideline us. The inner child that wants to be part of the action will encourage us in our daily races.

Lord, help me parent my inner child as You parent me.

58

Extremes

Give me neither poverty nor riches, but give me only my daily bread. Otherwise, I may have too much and disown you and say, "Who is the Lord?" Or I may become poor and steal, and so dishonor the name of my God. (vv. 8-9)

Take it to the limit. A fast car, a relationship, the volume on a radio. We live in a time of extremes. State lottery games thrive on this human drive. I find this inclination spilling over into my spiritual perspective:

If poor is good, to have absolutely nothing is true spirituality.

If financial security is good, lots of money must mean you are really God's favored.

If self-control is good, self-deprivation must be better; inflicting pain must really show God you are serious.

If God gives us richly all things to enjoy then He approves of gluttony.

"Do not add to his words, or he will rebuke you and prove you a liar" (30:6). We so easily add to God's words and pretend to read into God's mind our own wishes. Agur, the sage writing this passage, reminds us that God's Word is flawless and without dross. It is as gold smelted in the furnace. We need not doubt His

Word or think His instruction needs our finishing touch or improvement.

Agur graphically describes God as beyond any extreme we can imagine. Can you envision gathering the wind in the palm of your hand? Or wrapping up all the waters of the world in your cloak? Keeping this perspective about God inspires us to conform to His direction without changing the blueprint.

We hear of leaders whose behavior slanders the name of God. They became so engrossed in fleshing out their extreme interpretation of spirituality that they lose sight of God, who holds the winds of the world in His hands. Becoming drunk on self-made extremes—poverty, loyalty, pain, or riches—forces God into the background and allows insatiable appetite to take control.

Working women may be drawn to extremes. The workaholic sacrifices personal relaxation and relationships in order to work long hours. Periodically, different areas of our lives demand extra attention, but we need frequently to evaluate our work, relationships, and special interests. The balance is easily tipped. Moderation escapes us at every opportunity.

God has a remedy for our tendency to live in extremes. "He who conceals his sins does not prosper, but whoever confesses and renounces them finds mercy" (28:13). We can be sure that as we submit each area of our lives to God, there will be an accompanying battle, maybe not to take back the new territory, but to push the borders to the limit, and in so doing to dishonor God's name.

That can happen to evangelists, counselors, broadcasters, salespersons, and accountants. Realizing this, we need to stay daily in the Word to experience the continual balance of our behavior against the Word of God.

When I sense my desire to push limits I read Psalm 119. For me, the outstanding characteristic of this psalm is its power to help us focus on the Word. "I have hidden your word in my heart that I might not sin against you" (v. 11). "I will walk about in freedom, for I have sought out your precepts" (v. 45). As I was strolling down a neighborhood road, a large dog charged from behind a garage. I was obviously threatening his territory and therefore became his target. He stopped abruptly in a grove of trees at the edge of the road and stood barking as if he were on a leash. He wore a small box on his collar. Protection had come from an invisible source, a hidden electronic fence controlled by his collar. God's Word is protection: visible, doable, safe in its limit setting. His limits are good for others and good for me.

Lord, if I push any limit,
may it be to be near You.

59
Weakness

*Four things on earth are small, yet they are ex-
tremely wise: Ants are creatures of little strength,
yet they store up their food in the summer; coneys are creatures of little power, yet they make
their home in the crags; locusts have no king, yet
they advance together in ranks; a lizard can be
caught with the hand, yet it is found in kings' pa-
laces. (vv. 24-28)*

Have you ever felt that success in the marketplace
is only for the strong or the powerful? God created all
kinds of people, both weak and strong. Why? Did He
intend that some would always have the advantage over
others? I think not. He gives us lessons from the ant,
the locust, the coney, and the lizard that are especially
helpful to working women.

There are four counterparts to weakness. We are
not to despise the weak things of the world; they are
offset by provision, sanctuary, order, and audacity.

The ant stores for the future and is industrious.
Ants work though they have no leader. They may appear to be racing meaninglessly in different directions,
but this is not the case. They are self-starters, initia-
tors who search out provisions to supply their colony.
We can imitate their initiative and future orientation.

Coneys are rock-badgers. They are similar to a
marmot. Their coat is a dull, fawn color, and they are

about the size of rabbits. Coneys post sentries who signal when danger approaches. They are shy and quick to retreat to their rock crevices. They make eagle territory their home because they know when to hide and use their habitat for their safety. We do well to recognize not only what we can do but what we cannot do.

Locusts have no king, but they function together like an orchestra. Locusts can move across a field, cleaning it better than expensive harvesting equipment. The seventeen-year locust appears in concert. When they emerged from the ground in our suburb, the noise of the local airport was drowned by their hum. Even phone conversations were difficult. Their ranks were thick; we could remove a garbage can full of locust shells every day from our driveway alone. The weakness of the locust is offset by his acting in concert; numbers plus cooperation becomes his strength. Similarly, through cooperation and networking we can work through our organization. Our size can be offset by numbers.

The lizard, though he can be held in the hand, is not awed by the most awesome setting. He is comfortable in a palace, on the tiles of a luxurious estate, or in the patio of an exotic hotel. Be it audacity or spiritedness, he is bold despite his small size. Working women need not sense intimidation. Remember whose daughter you are.

Solomon wrote, "I have seen something else under the sun: The race is not to the swift, or the battle to the strong, nor does food come to the wise or wealth to the brilliant or favor to the learned; but time and chance happen to them all" (Ecclesiastes 9:11). A person without God thinks time and change are chaotic; what will be will be. Christians trust the God-factor. The prophet Jahaziel told King Jehoshaphat, "For the battle is not yours, but God's" (2 Chronicles 20:15b). How true. Strength and power do not have the last word, God does.

When we feel insignificant in our marketplace and small in our circumstances, we can be encouraged by the industrious ant, the sanctuary-seeking coney, the orderly locust, and the bold lizard. Our weakness does not determine the outcome.

Lord, help me glory in my weakness as Paul did because Your strength is sufficient.

60
Character

Charm is deceptive, and beauty is fleeting; but a woman who fears the Lord is to be praised. Give her the reward she has earned, and let her works bring her praise at the city gate. (vv. 30-31)

If the best of Mary and Martha could be combined into one woman, here she is. Tradition says she may have been Solomon's mother, Bathsheba. We do not know. She sets a high standard that is beyond some of us. She is unusually gifted, a multi-talented person with considerable resources. Yet even though my gifts, talents, and resources are fewer, I have access to the same foundation: the fear and wisdom of God.

Let's look at what she built on that foundation. She had servants to manage and money to invest, over which she had sole responsibility. "She considers a field and buys it" (v. 16). She used her mind. She made decisions. Sometimes we feel we must rely on someone else's thinking and final word. Wise women seek a broad spectrum of advice, but then they make decisions and act. That is part of God's image in us. He can give wisdom to anyone—including you and me.

The advantages this woman experienced she used to widen her responsibilities rather than to become idle (v. 27), to help the poor rather than to become stingy (v. 20), and to prepare for the future rather than to become careless (v. 25). We would do well to model her. Consider the paycheck possibilities. What can I do to widen my responsibilities? Investing in new training may be a possibility. What might I do to help the poor who are unable to work? Will my dollar decision today hurt or help tomorrow? Consider your sphere of influence, your power. Our model used her talents instead of hiding them. We should follow suit.

In her thrift, she is not harsh, sour, or severely simple. She and her household are clothed in scarlet, fine linen, and purple. Those fabrics denote high cost, the best. "Adequate" is not the word for them. Quality is affordable to her. She wins the never-ending battle of deciding "How much?" When does frugality become stinginess? When does quality become conspicuous consumption? God desires a balance somewhere between the extremes of maxed-out credit cards and flea-market mentality. This woman had found the balance and lived confidently with God's blessing.

Though Proverbs 31 does not describe her relationships, we may assume they are positive. Others praise her and call her blessed, and she brings respect to her significant others.

She is to be given the reward she has earned and given that reward in public. We Christian working women must recognize that this may not happen to us in this life. Someone else at work may get the reward we earned. As Solomon discovered, time and circumstances affect us all. This is earth, not heaven. Wisdom is leaving not just the results in God's hands but also the rewards.

Lord, creating me was Your work, not mine.
I accept my weakness and strength as from Your hand.
Thank You for this model.
Though I ask You for many things and much help,
I plead most of all for wisdom.